A MIGRATION AUDIT OF POVERTY REDUCTION STRATEGIES IN SOUTHERN AFRICA

Benjamin Roberts

MIDSA Report No 3

Series Editors: Prof. Jonathan Crush and Vincent Williams

Acknowledgements

SAMP and IOM wish to acknowledge the editorial contribution of Dave Dorey and Bruce Frayne and the financial support of the UK Department for International Development (DFID) and the Human Sciences Research Council (HSRC).

Published by Idasa, 6 Spin Street, Church Square, Cape Town, 8001, and Queen's University, Canada.

© Southern African Migration Project (SAMP) 2007
ISBN 1-920118-45-4

First published 2007
Produced by Idasa Publishing

Table of Contents

List of Tables

Chapter 1
INTRODUCTION

Southern Africa is characterized by long-established patterns of intra-regional migration, with countries sending and receiving labour migrants especially for employment in mines and on commercial farms and plantations since the late nineteenth century.[1] However, these patterns and processes have undergone notable change in recent decades, the outcome being a progressive intensification of mobility in the region. The underlying determinants of this trend include increased and new opportunities for internal and cross-border movement following the end of apartheid, the region's increasing engagement with the global economy, persistently high and worsening levels of poverty and unemployment, the impact of the HIV/AIDS pandemic, and the displacement and forced migration borne out of conflict and civil strife.[2]

These changing dynamics are occurring at a time when there is an increasing recognition of and desire to understand the multifaceted and complex relationship between migration, livelihoods and poverty. This coincides with the emergence of a 'New Poverty Agenda', which builds upon the 1990 and 2000 World Development Reports and reflects the concern with poverty reduction as an integral part of the international development paradigm.[3] At the international level, the Millennium Development Goals form an important expression of this agenda. Similarly, since 1999, Poverty Reduction Strategy Papers (PRSPs) have become the most noteworthy policy instruments in low income countries to emanate from the new poverty agenda.

The principal objective of this paper is to examine the extent to which recent poverty reduction strategies and policy in Southern Africa reflect the current understanding of migration and its dynamics. This is of particular relevance since such policies, either directly or indirectly, can promote, accommodate or inhibit population mobility as well as affect the experiences of those who move and stay behind.[4] The analysis also provides some insight into the prevailing assumptions about migration and development of regional organizations, governments and donors that have shaped poverty reduction strategies in the sub-region.

This audit is organised into four chapters. Chapter 2 provides a content analysis of migration in SADC's Regional Indicative Strategic Development Plan (RISDP, 2004). The next chapter examines the seven low-income SADC countries that have adopted the World Bank/IMF Poverty Reduction Strategy Paper approach and shows how migration issues are dealt with in their PRSPs. The report then provides an analysis of how migration has been incorporated in the general poverty reduction strategies of middle-income countries. Based on the results of the audit, the final chapter identifies the issues and considerations necessary to effectively mainstream migration in ongoing poverty reduction strategies in Southern Africa, at the provincial, national and regional levels.

Study Approach

The study is a review of the recently completed Regional Indicative Strategic Development Plan for the SADC region, the Poverty Reduction Strategy Papers and national poverty reduction strategies produced by countries in the region, and other relevant documentation. In terms of the assessment framework used for the analysis, this report examines three dimensions of the mainstreaming of migration. The first is the extent to which migration issues have been described in the poverty profile or situational analysis contained in the strategy documents. These profiles aim to identify the nature and causes of poverty, and are natural focal points for the inclusion of specific concerns and opportunities pertaining to migration. The focus is on identifying analytical and structural gaps. Secondly, the extent to which the links between migration and poverty have been incorporated into this contextual analysis is addressed. The third and final dimension is the degree of sensitivity to migration issues in the policy and programmatic responses that are formulated to address national poverty situations and challenges. This entails a reasonably comprehensive review of the sector-based priorities or focus areas that collectively form the basis of poverty reduction strategies. This review will also assess whether mobile populations are specifically targeted and whether they are recognised as a means of poverty reduction.

Chapter

REGIONAL POVERTY REDUCTION POLICY FRAMEWORK

2

The SADC Regional Indicative Strategic Development Plan

The SADC Regional Indicative Strategic Development Plan (RISDP) was officially launched on 12 March 2004 during the proceedings of a two-day Southern African Development Community (SADC) Council of Ministers meeting in Arusha, Tanzania.[5] The Plan represents the key policy framework for operationalising the SADC Common Agenda and guiding regional economic integration and social development over the next 15 years. It therefore lays out the framework within which SADC institutions, member states, regional stakeholders and international cooperating partners will combine efforts to implement specific programmes, policies and strategies aimed at attaining the region's overarching goal of eliminating poverty.

The RISDP is informed by a regional situation analysis of recent economic, human and social trends and a review of existing policies and strategies. Despite economic improvements in the 1990s, several countries experienced low and decreasing per capita gross national income, low growth rates of gross domestic product, relatively high budget deficits and interest rates, relatively low savings and investment rates and high external debt burdens. These factors have contributed to high levels of poverty in the region. It has been estimated that GNI per capita must grow at approximately 10% (and GDP at more than 7%) if the Millennium Development Goal (MDG) of halving poverty by 2015 is to be attained. While the level of human development improved in some countries in the mid-to-late 1990s, it declined in the majority of countries. This is attributable to reduced life expectancy at birth, decreases in real per capita incomes and reversals in school enrolment rates. The Southern African region is therefore confronted with relatively high levels of poverty, high HIV prevalence rates, rising illiteracy in some countries and shortages of critical human skills, among other challenges. The RISDP deems previous policy responses and programmatic interventions as rather ineffectual, given their limited impact on regional integration and development.

Based on an assessment of the gaps and challenges in pre-existing policies and strategies, the RISDP identifies priority intervention areas for the region, each of which is presented with an overall goal, areas of focus, key strategies and broad targets. The main intervention areas of the RISDP are divided into two main groups:

- Cross-Sectoral Intervention Areas: poverty eradication; combating the HIV/AIDS pandemic; gender equality and development; science and technology; information and communications technology; environment and sustainable development; private sector development; and statistics.

- Sectoral Cooperation and Integration Intervention Areas: trade/economic liberalisation and development; infrastructure support for regional integration and poverty eradication; sustainable food security; and human and social development.

In selecting long-term development targets and indicators to monitor progress in each of the RISDP priority intervention areas, attention has been paid to ensuring consistency with the international agreements and initiatives to which Member States have committed themselves. These include the Millennium Declaration and the associated Millennium Development Goals (MDGs) and the New Partnership for Africa's Development (NEPAD) priority areas.

Institutionally, the RISDP proposes a three-tiered framework. At the political level, the Council of Ministers through the Integrated Committee of Ministers (ICM) will provide policy direction and oversight to implementation. At the operational level, the SADC Secretariat will assume primary responsibility for management and coordination. As for the implementation of particular programmes, the principle of subsidiarity has been adopted.[6] Accordingly, all programmes and activities should be decided on and undertaken at the national and local levels whenever possible, with regional actions only when there are clear benefits to be gained that could not be realised at a lower level. This means that Member States are mainly responsible for the initiation and implementation of programmes, though a number of additional supporting structures have been proposed, including Technical Advisory Committees and Sub-committees (technical guidance and quality control), Programme Steering Committees, and SADC National Committees (information dissemination, monitoring, and ensuring inclusive consultations).

The successful implementation of the RISDP is contingent upon the mobilisation of sufficient resources on a sustainable basis over the 15 year period. The financial resources strategy in the RISDP expects it to be funded from increased Member State contributions and grants from international development partners. The plan also emphasizes the need for improvements in national public expenditure management, the functional use and effective application of foreign aid, and the pursuance of effective debt relief strategies.[7]

To ensure that the plan remains a 'living' document that is periodically updated, the principles of flexibility and adaptability are stressed.[8] Provision has also been made for continuous monitoring and evaluation of progress towards the targets. An integrated monitoring system will be established, to be coordinated by the SADC Secretariat at the regional level and SADC National Committees at the national level. Annual progress and evaluation reports will be prepared, with an independent in-depth evaluation of the implementation of the RISDP every three years.[9] This evidence base will be used to refine and increasingly focus strategies and introduce new interventions where necessary.

The SADC needs to be commended on its commitment to developing a framework for addressing intractable poverty and inequality in the region. However, the difficult question that inevitably has to be asked is to what extent the plan represents a roadmap that accommodates the differential levels of development in the region and articulates the specific set of interventions that will be needed to fulfil the regional long-term vision? The strategies for meeting the goals and areas of focus within each of the priority areas also suffer from a lack of specificity. Yet, as indicated in the following extract, the document is emphatic about its role as a supportive framework for poverty reduction in the region rather than a narrowly defined suite of interventions:

> The RISDP is indicative in nature and outlines the necessary conditions that should be realised towards the attainment of SADC's regional integration and development goals. In other words, it is not a prescriptive or a command type of plan. In view of the need to monitor and measure progress, the RISDP sets targets that indicate major milestones towards the attainment of agreed goals. In this connection, the RISDP sets up a logical and coherent implementation programme of the main activities necessary for the achievement of the region's broader goals with a reasonable, feasible and agreeable time frame that takes into account resource constraints.[10]

Nonetheless, while the plan may impart a sense of the strategic direction that member states and regional institutions need to follow over the next fifteen years, it is important that regional policymakers attempt to resolve the specificity problem as part of the implementation planning process. As a logical first step, more explicit reference should be made to the measures being advocated by the protocols which underpin it. This would enable a more robust and informed debate about the adequacy of this suite of measures to achieve the stated goals and targets. A failure to do so is likely to frustrate the effective implementation of the Plan. Fortunately, it appears that there is general recognition of the urgent need to unbundle the plan and allocate clear and specific roles to key-players with quantifiable deliverables:

> The RISDP is, in a sense, a strategic framework pointing the general direction the Region would like to move. Concrete time bound and costed activities/programmes/projects will be developed and clearly spelt out in implementation/action plans for each project/programme. This will be done immediately after the appropriate SADC authorities have approved the broad strategic framework.[11]

The intention is that this planning and prioritizing of specific activities in the main intervention areas will be undertaken by SADC's Department of Strategic Planning, Gender and Policy Harmonisation.[12]

The Representation of Migration in the RISDP

While regional integration and cooperation in the region is a strong focus of the Plan, there is limited discussion of migration and its connection to development. Migration has also not been included among the prioritised intervention areas in the RISDP. Instead, it features implicitly as a cross-cutting issue in the document. Examples include the need to: (a) remove obstacles to cross-border trade and investment; (b) establish mechanisms for the movement of labour and (c) develop intra-regional tourism by easing or removing travel and visa restrictions and harmonising immigration procedures.[13] Apart from these illustrations, migration is acknowledged as a stress factor that, together with poverty and unemployment, encourages desperate income-generating activities, such as the production and trafficking of illicit drugs.[14]

One of the few places in the Plan where migration is dealt with explicitly is in relation to the cross-border and international migration of skilled Africans – the 'brain drain' phenomenon. The document observes that a major challenge for the SADC region is the loss of educated and skilled health and teaching professionals due to better opportunities abroad and the devastating impact of the HIV/AIDS pandemic.[15] The plan goes on to articulate four strategies that will be pursued by SADC in order to keep and utilize skills:

- Harmonising policies and programmes for employment creation, income generation and productivity improvement with a view to enhancing the labour-absorptive capacity of the national economies as well as measures to reduce the brain drain in the region and mitigate the impact of the HIV/AIDS pandemic on the workforce;

- Harmonising policies and facilitating the establishment of mechanisms for the movement of labour;

- Developing a policy framework for the facilitation of cross-border informal trade for employment creation and income generation;

- Coordinating policies and strategies to enhance and strengthen infrastructure for the constant flow and dissemination of information.[16]

While these may be laudable as far as policy objectives go, they suffer from a lack of specificity. For instance, it is not clear what policy mechanisms are being advocated to retain skilled workers within national economies in the region. This raises the question of how the 'push' factors will be addressed so that skilled workers can be encouraged to stay, especially in low income countries and in under-serviced rural enclaves. Importantly, the Plan recognises the existence of highly differentiated resource availability across the region.

Similarly, regional efforts to regulate labour migration over the last decade have met with limited success. The SADC *Draft Protocol on the Facilitation of Movement of Persons*, which has been through an iterative process of revision, envisages the progressive realisation of the free movement of persons between SADC member states, including the right to seek employment, to be employed and to reside in any member state. Yet, a consensus among member states on the adoption of the protocol has yet to be reached.[17] Absent this consensus, it remains unclear how the RISDP, in advocating a relaxation of immigration laws and facilitation of movement of people between countries in the region, intends to achieve this elusive goal and move the process of regional integration forward.

The apparent lack of recognition in the RISDP of the importance of migration as a potential poverty mitigation strategy, coupled with evidence of mounting cross-border mobility, makes it imperative that regional development strategies take cognisance of the role of migration in the development process. A failure to do so may serve to undermine the efficacy of such policies and associated programmatic interventions in addressing the core MDG of significant poverty reduction by 2015.

Importance of Migration to the Intervention Areas

While migration is not substantively addressed in the RISDP, many of the priority intervention areas identified in the document cannot be discussed without taking account of migration. In order for programmatic interventions to achieve the desired poverty-reducing effect in the region in the medium to long-term, there is an urgent need for regional policymakers to recognise the inextricable role that migration plays. This section therefore provides a discussion of the close relationship between a select number of the RISDP priority intervention areas and human mobility. Six intervention areas are indicated by the plan as being particularly salient in efforts to reduce poverty in the region:

Poverty eradication is addressed in all intervention areas

outlined...in particular, in the priority intervention areas of combating of the HIV/AIDS pandemic; gender equality and development; trade, economic liberalisation and development; infrastructure support for regional integration and poverty eradication; sustainable food security; and in human and social development.[18]

Combating the HIV/AIDS pandemic

Population mobility has always been a major driving force in epidemics of infectious disease.[19] Research has shown that there exists a strong link between various kinds of mobility and heightened risk of HIV and migration has come to be regarded as one of the characteristics of a risk environment in which individuals and groups are highly susceptible to HIV.[20] Therefore, given the exceptionally high rates of population movement both within and between countries in Southern Africa, it is unsurprising that migration has played a significant role in the rapid transmission of HIV in the region.

Across the region, the predominant pattern is still of men migrating to urban centres in search of work, leaving their partners and children at home in rural areas and returning on a periodic basis depending on the distances involved.[21] This form of male circular migration is the result of a complex interplay of historical, political, economic, environmental and demographic factors.[22] Many migrants move from low HIV prevalence areas to those with higher prevalence, which increases their risk of being exposed to the virus. Most studies that have been conducted focus on the migration of men and the risk involved for them and their non-migrant partners. For instance, in one study in a rural district of KwaZulu-Natal, South Africa, HIV prevalence was found to be twice as high among migrant workers (26%) than among non-migrant workers.[23]

It is important to look beyond this type of movement to other forms of migration, each of which may carry different levels of risk for acquiring and spreading HIV and other sexually transmitted infections in the region. Female migration is a smaller and much less-documented phenomenon. Nonetheless, the circular migration of women is increasing and poses similar risks as for men, with migrant women at significantly higher risk of HIV infection than non-migrant women.[24] Forced migration, often as a result of political conflict or instability, has produced large numbers of refugees in Southern Africa. These situations can result in rapid increases in HIV risk as people are forced to flee their homes and communities.[25]

The wide variety of conditions facing migrants in the region requires that HIV prevention be carefully tailored to the specific circumstances of different groups. In Southern Africa mobile groups include truck drivers, cross-border traders, mineworkers, construction workers, farmworkers, domestic workers, sex workers, military personnel and refugees.[26] Internationally, attention has increasingly focused on prevention among mobile populations that regularly cross international borders. As many as 56 such programmes are in operation in Africa.[27]

Many HIV/AIDS policies have been introduced in the SADC region, including strategic plans, codes of conduct, as well as workplace and sectoral policies. However, a recent review of the HIV/AIDS policies of eight SADC member states found that only two – Lesotho and Zambia – included mobile populations as a vulnerable group in their national strategic plans.[28] At the sectoral level, some countries have HIV/AIDS policies that apply to those sectors in which mobile populations are employed (e.g. agriculture, minerals and energy, transport, public works and uniformed services), yet these rarely discuss the underlying causes of vulnerability facing such groups.[29] One of the key lessons to emerge from this research in the region is the need for mobile populations to be integrated into national and sectoral plans on HIV/AIDS, and for the introduction of strategies specifically designed for these vulnerable groups, in order for the spread of AIDS to be halted or even begin to be reversed by 2015.

HIV/AIDS policies and strategies at the regional level should similarly aim to address the specific needs and rights of mobile groups. The SADC *Code of Conduct on HIV/AIDS and Employment* is considered particularly relevant in this regard. Amongst other things, it opposes compulsory workplace HIV testing, and calls instead for the removal of restrictions on family reunification (allowing labour migrants to move with their families and dependants) and provision of the means to minimize the risk of infection such as information, condoms and adequate accommodation.[30] Surprisingly, the RISDP does not mention mobile populations as vulnerable groups. It instead refers generically to the need to reduce the incidence of HIV and AIDS among the most vulnerable groups. In addition, it does not make reference to the code of conduct, but does refer to the SADC Multi-sectoral HIV and AIDS Strategic Framework and Programme of Action 2003-2007.

Apart from the vulnerability of mobile populations to HIV/AIDS-related migration, the pandemic is also beginning to exert an influence on migration patterns. For example, AIDS-affected children in Southern Africa have been shown to migrate when household members fall sick or die from AIDS, or because they are sent to assist relatives.[31] In Lesotho and Malawi, there is evidence suggesting that children sent to live with kin commonly move over long distances and between urban and rural areas. Difficulties associated with such movements include having to integrate into new families and communities, and the severing of family ties which can lead to children ending up in institutions or on the streets.[32] Policymakers therefore need to be responsive to these newly-emerging vulnerable groups.

Gender Equality and Development

Gender relations are an important dimension of migration. In many societies, gender relations have been characterized by an unequal balance of power, with women having less access than men to education, training and resources.[33] Traditional views on the roles and responsibilities of women have meant that they continue to serve as primary caregivers, fulfilling reproductive and (unpaid) domestic functions such as housework, fetching and heating water, cooking, and caring for children, old people and sick people. This, in turn, has constrained their access to education, training, land and productive assets, as well as restricted the time available for paid productive work and the choice of income-earning activities.[34] These socio-cultural practices have resulted in women conventionally becoming de facto household heads, dependent on remittances from male labour migrants.

However, these patterns have not remained static, and declining real wages and employment prospects over the last couple of decades have had a major impact on livelihoods and migration strategies.[35] Of particular relevance are the new social, spatial and temporal patterns that have begun to emerge due to an increasing number of women engaging in internal and cross-border migration in Southern Africa.[36]

As Table 1 indicates, the proportion of females among international migrants in Africa has generally been lower than the global average.

Even so, there has been steady feminisation of international migration on the continent. Southern Africa has traditionally had the lowest proportion of females among the international migrant stock (42% in 2005 up from 30% in 1960). The traditional reliance of the mining industry on male migrant workers was largely responsible for this pattern. Since the 1980s, retrenchments and mine closures in the mining sector have resulted in a gradual decline in the number of temporary migrant workers employed and an increase in the proportion of women in the overall international migrant stock.[37]

One example of this feminisation of migration comes from the small, landlocked kingdom of Lesotho. The recent expansion of the clothing and textiles sector under the African Growth and Opportunity Act (AGOA) has prompted an increasing feminisation of internal migration in the country.[38] Women are also making a growing proportion of the migrant population crossing into South Africa.[39]

Despite the feminisation of migration, persisting gender inequalities exert a strong influence over the availability and nature of livelihood opportunities for women. Limited educational attainment confines many of them to gender-segregated and unregulated sectors of the economy, such as informal trade, domestic work or sex work.[40] Furthermore, many women are in unskilled jobs, earn low wages, work long hours, have little or no job security or rights to social benefits and face limited prospects for upward mobility. These forms of employment also render women more vulnerable to human rights abuses, harassment and violence since they are not protected by labour legislation or policy.[41]

Table 1: Proportion Female Among International Migrants, 1960-2000						
Region	1960	1970	1980	1990	2000	2005
World	46.8	47.1	47.2	49.0	49.7	49.6
More developed regions	48.9	48.9	49.8	52.0	52.1	52.2
Less developed regions	45.3	45.8	44.8	45.7	46.1	45.5
Africa	42.3	42.7	44.1	45.9	47.2	47.4
Eastern Africa	41.9	43.2	45.3	47.3	47.9	48.3
Middle Africa	44.0	45.5	45.8	46.0	46.2	46.3
Northern Africa	49.5	47.7	45.8	45.6	44.4	43.6
Southern Africa	30.1	30.3	35.6	38.7	41.3	42.4
Western Africa	42.1	43.0	43.5	46.4	48.8	49.0
Asia	46.4	46.8	44.6	45.2	45.4	44.7
Latin America and the Caribbean	44.7	46.8	48.2	49.7	50.2	50.3
Northern America	50.5	51.5	52.6	51.0	50.4	50.4
Europe	48.4	47.7	48.1	52.8	53.4	53.4
Oceania	44.4	46.5	47.9	49.1	50.6	51.3
Source: World Migrant Stock, The 2005 Population Revision Database, UN ESA http://esa.un.org/migration/ Accessed Dec. 18, 2006.						

Migration also tends to render women more vulnerable to the sexual transmission of HIV infection.[42] The partners of male migrants are at a high risk of HIV infection when their partners return home regularly from areas of high HIV prevalence. These women are also confronted with situations where, in the absence of partners and regular remittances, they may have to sell or trade sex in order to survive.

The increasing feminisation of internal and international migration has meant that gender issues are receiving significantly more attention in migration literature and research. However, in spite of the increased focus on women's rights and the special needs of female migrants, policy has tended to lag behind and needs to reflect a greater awareness and understanding of the conditions and needs of migrant women.[43] By way of example, migration-related policies and regulations have yet to adjust to the reality that population movements can be highly gender-specific. Women and men migrate for diverse reasons along different routes and with different outcomes.[44] Gender analysis has also shown that there are gender differences in terms of migrant labour, and motives for remitting.[45] Since policies that neglect the gendered nature of migration can yield unanticipated costs for women, it is important that policymakers begin to develop migration policy that will facilitate rather than hinder female migratory flows.

Trade/Economic Liberalisation and Development

Much attention has been, and continues to be, devoted to formal sector regional trade patterns in Southern Africa. While these intra-regional trade flows are significant, especially as SADC heads toward the establishment of a Free Trade Area by 2008, a complex network of informal sector cross-border trade also exists in the region.[46] The evidence suggests that it represents a sizable share of cross-border trade in the region, and involves the exchange of large volumes of commodities, most notably food and agricultural goods.[47] In addition, cross-border trade within Southern Africa is a household livelihood strategy and plays a contributory role in ensuring household (and indeed regional) food security. Women are well-represented in the ranks of informal sector cross-border traders whose economic activities provide important income-earning opportunities.[48]

Regional informal cross-border traders are often confronted with major bureaucratic and other barriers. They therefore have to negotiate migratory legislative frameworks as well as customs and excise policies. One study of informal cross-border traders in South Africa revealed the heavy time and financial burdens involved in procuring visitors visas and paying customs duties.[49] High customs duties erode limited profit margins, which in turn reduces the ability of traders to trade across borders and encourages attempts to beat the system. Weaknesses in customs administration also mean unofficial rents and the harassment of informal traders.[50] The obstacles informal cross-border traders face have an explicit gender dimension. For instance, women entrepreneurs tend to be more exposed to risk than their male counterparts as they often cannot afford safer and more secure modes of transportation, are more vulnerable to abuse and exploitation by customs officials, and are at greater risk of sexual violence.[51]

The activities of cross-border traders have tended to be overlooked in migration legislation as well as regional and national trade policies.[52] The RISDP does acknowledge the importance of the informal cross-border trade, describing it as 'substantial', 'thriving throughout the region' and a livelihood source for 'a large proportion of the population.'[53] Moreover, the Plan asserts that current 'SADC trade policies and strategies are consistent with the objectives of eliminating obstacles to the free movement of capital, labour and goods and services.'[54] Yet it also concedes that one of the trade-related challenges in the region is to 'develop new policies and strategies that would target vulnerable groups such as the rural and urban poor, small businesses, informal operators and women.'[55] More specifically, it mentions that 'in developing the policies and strategies for industrial and mining development, the question of the informal sector, both in terms of trade liberalization and actual production, should be taken on board.'[56]

The architects of the RISDP thus provide some indication that the concerns of informal cross-border traders are important, but a number of questions and concerns remain. The Plan has been conceived as a mechanism for providing strategic direction for SADC programmes and activities vis-à-vis long-term development objectives. It is critical, however, to ensure that the trade policies and protocols underpinning the RISDP framework sufficiently encompass and actively promote the activities of small, medium and micro-enterprises or informal sector traders and their role in cross-border trade. This is especially necessary given the role of these traders in household livelihood security, gender empowerment and poverty alleviation.

Infrastructural Support for Regional Integration and Poverty Eradication

High unemployment rates in the region may create a situation where access to infrastructure becomes a factor influencing migration decision-making. Moving to centres that offer relatively better access to services and mass transport may allow households to reduce transport costs and labour time loss. Other deciding factors may include access to land, security of tenure, job opportunities, transport and services infrastructure (schools and clinics), basic needs infrastructure (water and electricity), free natural resources and personal safety.[57] In a South African study, infrastructure was the second-ranked attractor of migration behind employment in KwaZulu-Natal, and third-ranked for the Eastern Cape.[58]

In spite of this, migrants are often less able to access services than the local population in destination areas because they have fewer rights and often an unclear legal status. This can play a major role in shaping the impact of migration. Many may end up residing in informal settlements or slums where they are unable to connect to electricity, water and sanitation infrastructure. Access to secure land and housing may also be circumscribed.

Intensifying processes of urbanisation place increasing pressure on existing services, threatening advances that had been achieved over the past twenty years. For example, while 77% of households in Lesotho lacked access to adequate sanitation in 1987, this had been dramatically reduced to 48% by 1995.[59] The number of households gaining access to adequate sanitation had more than doubled, which has been attributed to the success of the national sanitation programme.[60] Access to sanitation improved significantly for rural households and kept apace with the rate of progress required to fulfil the 2015 MDG target. Despite these remarkable gains, a slight overall worsening occurred in the late 1990s. The downturn can be traced to a rapid increase in the urban population and uncontrolled urban sprawl, which make it difficult to provide and maintain essential services.

The development of infrastructure also has the capacity to enhance the potential of remittances to reduce poverty by enabling migrants to maintain closer connections with people back home. For example, improving access to financial services to the rural poor may help foster a situation where remittances can be easily invested, rather than simply received and spent on basic commodities. Developing partnerships between banks, other financial institutions, microfinance organisations and post offices may therefore promote the development impact of remittances. Such services are dependent on the availability of a strong supportive infrastructure such as reliable electricity supply, decent roads and other communications resources.[61]

These intersections between migration and infrastructure have significant implications for public spending, for development delivery and for transformation and social justice at the national and regional level.[62] While improved service delivery in poor, rural source areas would facilitate the creation of livelihood opportunities and possibly slow down the rate of population movement, the cost of rural infrastructure remains high. Focusing on rapidly densifying destination areas may be logistically easier and cheaper (at least in the short term), but this would perpetuate geographic inequalities and result in an increasing strain on services in these areas in the short to medium term. It is therefore imperative that national and regional planners and policymakers consider, in determining infrastructural investment patterns, the effect that migration and changes in population distribution have upon the demand for services.

Return migration can inject financial resources and new skills into the local economy. However, the effect is generally limited and depends on the level of access to different forms of infrastructure in home areas. Settlements with good road and transport networks and which offer non-farm employment opportunities locally or within commuting distance attract much larger numbers of return migrants than remote settlements.[63]

Sustainable Food Security

Migration is important to accessing food for poor and vulnerable households.[64] As such, migration has emerged as a key dimension of the livelihood strategies adopted by a sizable proportion of rural households in Southern Africa. Remittances may contribute towards household food security by increasing cash incomes that assist in securing and smoothing food consumption levels.[65] A recent SAMP study found that many Swazi households with migrants in South Africa were highly dependent on remitted income to meet their minimum food requirements. Any disruption to this income source (especially due to restrictive migrant labour policy) would expose these households to great risk given the limited prospects of finding employment at home.[66]

Migration can adversely influence food production in home areas by removing labour but can have a positive effect if remittances are used to finance inputs and capital equipment.[67] Support for the long-term food security strategy of investing a share of remittance earnings to enhance crop production and the accumulation of livestock was found in Mozambique, Botswana, and Swaziland.[68] These social and economic linkages are not necessarily unidirectional in nature, with people and resources (money and goods) moving from urban to rural areas. In Namibia, while many urban households visit and send money to rural relatives, an estimated two-thirds of these households receive food from rural areas.[69]

A decline in migration options has been cited as one of the principal causes of rising vulnerability across the Southern African region. From the early 1990s onwards, the retrenchment or repatriation of migrant workers has caused a decline in official remittance income in the SADC region. In Malawi, Lesotho and Swaziland this has had a negative effect on rural cash incomes during the 1990s. In Mozambique, the effects have been overshadowed by the even more adverse legacy of the civil war. In Zimbabwe and Zambia, layoffs have been a significant contributory factor in shrinking the rural cash economy.[70]

Migration is often relied upon as a coping response to the disruption of food and cash crop production by periodic droughts and floods. During the recent humanitarian crisis in Southern Africa, some of the coping strategies that were identified include migration, sending children away from home, and prostitution.[71] In Zimbabwe, migration in search of food increased, with reported population movements into the highveld prime communal zone, as well as across the border into Tete Province, Mozambique. In Mozambique, survival strategies adopted in response to food scarcity include casual labour (locally or migratory) and seasonal migration to look for work in 'better off' neighbouring districts. Irregular migration from Lesotho into South Africa also showed an upward trend during the crisis, and approximately 30% of food insecure households reported temporary migration, in contrast with only 18% of food secure households. Moreover, a quarter of Basotho households identified as food insecure were sending children away to relatives or friends, compared with 9% of food secure households.

With few income earning options, women and girls are often forced into commercial sex work, an activity which may involve migration. As food insecurity prompts migration, exposure to HIV/AIDS also increases. Migration, prostitution and sending children away from home all represent coping strategies that increase HIV transmission rates.[72]

Human and Social Development

The prioritization of human and social development aims to reduce human poverty in the region and improve the availability of educated, skilled, healthy, flexible, culturally-responsive, productive and efficient human resources. This is seen as a necessary precondition for the promotion of equitable growth, deeper integration and the global competitiveness of SADC. The RISDP focuses on the development, sustenance and increasing utilisation of human capabilities, and the development of positive values, attitudes and practices. The proposed strategies include (a) coordination, harmonization and engendering of education, training, health, nutrition, employment and labour policies; (b) the harmonization of policies for employment creation and income generation; (c) and the establishment of exchange programmes and mechanisms for key stakeholders.

Health is a key development indicator and poor health and inadequate health services provide a barrier to the alleviation of poverty.[73] The effective functioning of healthcare systems is highly dependent upon the availability of skilled human resources. In Southern Africa, these systems are compromised by a limited number of health professionals. As Table 2 indicates, the availability of health personnel varies markedly between countries in the region, with a large number of countries not meeting the 'Health for All' standard of one doctor per 5,000 people (or 20 per 100,000). A decade later, the situation is even worse. Health staff vacancy rates are extremely high. Health workers are also inequitably distributed within countries, especially between public and private heath sectors, urban and rural areas and tertiary and primary levels of the health system.[74] In Tanzania, the nurse-per-100,000 population ratio in urbanized Dar es Salaam is 160, but in the rest of Tanzania there are districts with a ratio of fewer than 6 nurses per 100,000.[75]

Table 2: Estimates of Health Personnel per 100,000 Population					
Country	Year	Physicians	Nurses	Midwives	Dentists
South Africa	1996	56.3	471.8	n.a.	17.8
Namibia	1997	29.5	168.0	116.5	4.0
Botswana	1994	23.8	219.1	0.0	2.2
Swaziland	1996	15.1	n.a	n.a	n.a
Zimbabwe	1995	13.9	128.7	28.1	1.3
Angola	1997	7.7	114.5	4.3	0.0
Zambia	1995	6.9	113.1	n.a	n.a
D.R.C.	1996	6.9	44.2	n.a	1.1
Lesotho	1995	5.4	60.1	47.0	0.5
Tanzania	1995	4.1	85.2	44.8	0.7
Source: WHO estimates cited in Padarath et al., Health Personnel in Southern Africa (see note 74)					

Already overstretched health systems are being further constrained by the emigration of health professionals out of the region. This staff loss can be ascribed to factors such as the burden of increasing patient load, work-related risk of diseases like HIV/AIDS and TB, poor infrastructure and low staff morale.[76] Health workers are therefore faced with increasing emotional and physical strain and job dissatisfaction.[77] Additional exogenous factors include political insecurity, crime, high taxation levels and deteriorating standards of service. Under such circumstances, it is hardly surprising that health workers are lured by the prospects of improved quality of life, career opportunities and better wages and benefits in other countries.

Cumulatively, these migration trends have an immense impact on the capacity of the health care system to cope with the demand for health services, thus perpetuating and further exacerbating existing inequities. In a region that is characterised by some of the world's highest HIV prevalence rates, this capacity shortfall represents a critical impediment to programmatic interventions, such as the prospects for expanding access to antiretrovirals. For example, approximately 80 percent of 222 South African health care facilities recently surveyed said they needed additional staff to cope with the demand for HIV/AIDS services.[78]

The medical brain drain is most obvious to Australia, Canada, the Gulf countries, the United Kingdom and the United States. These countries offer an attractive alternative to the poor conditions and low pay that characterize SADC health-care systems. South Africa is particularly adversely affected by the out-migration of doctors and nurses seeking higher paying employment overseas.[79] Between 1989 and 1997, more than 82,000 health workers are estimated to have emigrated from South Africa.[80] The South African Medical Association has further estimated that as many as 5,000 doctors have left the country in recent years, while the Democratic Nursing Organization of South Africa has stated that 300 trained nurses leave each month. Zambia represents another hard-hit example, with only 400 practising doctors remaining in the country.[81]

A number of recent studies have begun to explore the policy options that would assist developing countries in coping with the effects that internal and international migration have on the quality, efficiency and effectiveness of health care systems. Two particularly relevant examples are outlined below.

One study on the migration of African health professionals to Canada, examines levels of support for different policy options to reduce or repair the brain drain.[82] Of the eight policy options presented to the Canadian respondents for consideration, improved planning for health human resources in Canada to reduce 'pull' factors received universal support. Similarly, most expressed some support for the adoption of a voluntary or mandatory code of practice, though some voiced concern about the risk of failure of such an approach due to the discretionary nature of the former and the demanding monitoring requirements of the latter. Strengthening health care systems in source countries to reduce 'push' factors secured some support, though it was acknowledged as being relatively low on the agenda of Canadian organizations. Ambivalent views were expressed towards bilateral or multilateral agreements to manage the migration of health professionals. The remaining options were virtually unanimously rejected, namely: reparation payments to source countries; increasing the numbers of auxiliary health care workers in source countries unlikely to gain entry into the Canadian labour market or be eligible for voluntary migration under Canada's immigration criteria; restrictions on the migration of health care professionals from underserved source countries into Canada; and bonding health care professionals in source countries to prevent their emigration for a period of time.

Another study by the World Health Organisation (WHO) draws on the experiences of six African countries and explores policies or strategies that have been adopted to either retain skilled health personnel or mitigate the effects of migration.[83] It argues that measures such as the use of foreign health personnel, bonding of newly qualified graduates, provision of more opportunities for professional advancement and periodical salary reviews have invariably failed to retain and attract new personnel to the public sector. Explanatory factors for this failure include a lack of improvement in health sector conditions (poor remuneration, working conditions and resources) and the piecemeal implementation of such approaches.[84] The report also calls for a more aggressive approach on the part of developing countries to prevent further attrition. Proposed measures include investing in comprehensive human resource information systems to provide reliable data on available human resources; providing realistic remuneration packages; improving general working conditions; offering non-financial incentives (e.g. training, study leave, opportunity to work in a team); and the bonding of skilled health professionals after qualification.[85] It further advocates bilateral agreements that would involve destination countries paying financial compensation to source countries and the provision of international fellowships or exchange programmes, as well as advocating the adoption of and compliance with codes of conduct pertaining to migration.

Although the two documents engage with a similar set of policy options, a comparison of the findings suggests the inherent difficulty in arriving at a consensus on how to mitigate the negative effects of skilled-labour migration. This is hardly surprising given that multiple stakeholders are involved, including employers in both the source and receiving countries, governments, and the international development community, each with potentially differing or competing perspectives on the matter. In such a context, determining who assumes responsibility for addressing the challenge posed by the migration of health professionals from Southern Africa becomes a deeply contested issue. For instance, in the Canadian study, compensation payments to source countries and bonding of health care professionals were options dismissed by the respondent organisations, whereas they were openly endorsed in the WHO report. While the disagreement on certain policy options is unlikely to be resolved in a timely manner, a failure to institute any measures may ultimately mean that the trend will continue unabated.

Education occupies a critical role in regional and national strategies for poverty reduction, human development and economic growth in Southern Africa, and the RISDP recognizes its importance. In order to survive, realise individual and social potential, participate in development and improve the quality of life, people need educational opportunities designed to meet their basic learning needs. Since labour is the principal asset of the poor, increasing the productivity of labour brings them direct rewards. Increasing access to schooling is also likely to reduce inter-generational inequalities in education.[86] The availability of well-trained and motivated teachers is critical to ensuring that these developmental goals are achieved. Yet, as with the health sector, migration is affecting both the supply of and demand for educational services. The loss of teaching professionals in the region may affect the ability of many governments to effectively provide schooling. The problem of staff retention is the result of a combination of teacher attrition and teacher transfers.[87]

The limited evidence on staff retention in schooling systems in Southern Africa suggests that teacher transfers between schools rather than attrition is the main source of turnover in most countries.[88] Dominant forms of teacher transfer include movements of teachers between public and non-state schools, and between primary and secondary schools, in addition to the taking of study leave in order to upgrade professional teaching qualifications. Turnover is especially rapid in hard-to-staff rural schools. A survey of 65 rural primary schools in Malawi found that nearly 25% of teachers had left their schools between January and October 1999.[89] Study leave may represent a key mechanism for career advancement, and many primary school teachers who upgrade their qualifications do not return to primary schools. In Tanzania, only half of the primary school teachers who upgraded during the 1990s returned to primary school teaching.[90]

With regard to teacher attrition, Ochs identifies five broad categories.[91] Firstly, teachers are actively recruited to developed nations, especially the United Kingdom, Canada, Australia and the United States, to meet teacher shortfalls. Second, teachers are recruited to developing (often neighbouring) countries. Third, teachers are 'drifting' to other countries to obtain qualifications, after which they decide to stay. Fourth, disaffection is encouraging teachers to leave the profession and take up other employment (occupational attrition). Finally, there is attrition due to retirement or death, the latter being increasingly related to HIV/AIDS.

Table 3: UK Work Permits for Teachers from Southern Africa, 2001-2003				
Country	2001	2002	2003	Total
South Africa	2010	2542	1492	6044
Zimbabwe	194	325	268	787
Mauritius	19	45	47	111
Zambia	16	22	16	54
Namibia	8	6	8	22
Seychelles	2	10	8	20
Malawi	3	10	4	17
Botswana	0	1	6	7
Tanzania	3	1	2	6
Swaziland	0	3	2	5
Regional sub-total	2255	2965	1853	7073
Total (all countries)	5064	7261	5564	17889
Share of total	44.5	40.8	33.3	39.5
Source: Adapted from Work Permits (UK); Bennell, Teaching Motivations (see note 90)				

Despite widespread concern over the 'brain drain' of educators to industrialised countries, the main impact on teacher supply in the SADC region is limited to certain countries, especially South Africa and Zimbabwe (Table 3).

Political and economic instability in Zimbabwe has led to a substantial outflow of teachers, though this should be regarded as an exceptional case in the region. The number of teachers leaving other countries in Southern Africa remains minimal. Reasons for the limited outflow from the region include falling demand for overseas teachers due to the large migration flows since the late 1990s, inadequate professional teaching qualifications of many primary school teachers and the circular nature of these flows, as many return after a few years abroad. As for intra-regional flows, Botswana and South Africa have found success in recruiting teachers from Zambia, Zimbabwe, and Ghana. However, the number of foreign migrant teachers in these countries has been levelling off.[92]

Some of the factors that encourage teacher mobility include; low salaries and benefits; the increasing roles and responsibilities teachers are expected to perform (including HIV/AIDS education, counselling and community development); the general decline in the status of teaching as an occupation in recent decades; and difficult working conditions (including large classes, limited resources, student behavioural problems, and long hours).[93] These circumstances have resulted in low teacher morale and the desire to find better employment opportunities and job satisfaction elsewhere.

Shifting briefly to the demand-side, migrant children (internal and cross-border) may change the spatial demand for educational services. The migration of children often reflects the mobility pattern of parents or the dynamics of child fostering.[94] Children of school-going age have also been shown to temporarily migrate due to the desire for better schooling.[95] This has the potential to place increasing pressure on educational facilities in receiving areas.

RISDP: Conclusions and Policy Implications

The preceding section provides an illustration of the extent to which migration underpins the Regional Indicative Strategic Development Plan's priority intervention areas, especially those that have been deemed central to the overarching goal of poverty reduction in Southern Africa. It is therefore disconcerting that the relationship between migration and poverty is under-represented in the plan's proposed intervention areas and only addressed in a partial and circumscribed manner. Southern Africa is a region on the move, with long-established, complex and increasingly dynamic patterns of migration and mobility. As such, attempting to understand contemporary regional development patterns without due consideration to the dynamic of migration is incomprehensible. Therefore, in developing its long-term strategic framework on regional integration and development, SADC has thus far missed the opportunity to draw from a range of lessons from national, regional and international experience, as well as recent advances in the understanding of the relationship between migration, poverty and development.

Migration needs to be regarded as more normal than exceptional, and an integral component of the livelihood strategies of numerous households in the region.[96] It therefore has the potential to make a substantive and positive contribution to poverty reduction. Certainly further policy development in the region needs to be based on a much more sophisticated understanding of the development-migration-poverty triangle. To ignore migration is to risk misinterpreting the way in which it can contribute to development in both source and recipient areas. Migration-blind policy thus risks missing opportunities for maximising beneficial development outcomes. As Skeldon notes, "policies that accept the wider mobility of the population are likely to accord with policies that will enhance the well-being of greater numbers of people."[97]

It is imperative that migration be systematically included in the ongoing process of translating the RISDP into a set of clearly defined policies, programmes, roles and responsibilities. Fortunately, the flexibilities built into the RISDP signify that there is a reasonably favourable prospect of ensuring that migration issues are not overlooked during the current rounds of planning and prioritizing in relation to the main intervention areas. In affording migration the centrality it deserves in regional policymaking, there is a need to go beyond a perfunctory recognition of its contribution to the development process. Policies should aim to enhance the contribution migration makes to the livelihoods of people, for instance by addressing xenophobia and discrimination against migrants and reducing unnecessary red tape.[98]

Chapter 3

NATIONAL PRSPs IN LOW-INCOME COUNTRIES

Poverty Reduction Strategy Papers (PRSPs): An Introduction

In late 1999, the World Bank and IMF announced that developing countries would in future need to complete Poverty Reduction Strategy Papers (PRSPs) as a precondition for accessing concessional finance and debt relief. Premised on the principles of national ownership, broad-based participation, comprehensiveness, pro-poor policy outcomes and a long-term perspective for poverty reduction, this new approach has rapidly become the dominant mechanism for development policy. This is especially true of Sub-Saharan Africa, where more than half the countries have either finalised or are in the process of preparing their poverty reduction strategies. Even countries that do not qualify for highly-indebted poor country (HIPC) or least-developed country (LDC) status have begun to voluntarily produce their own versions of the PRSP, and many other donors have decided to link their aid policies to the PRSP system.

Table 4: Poverty Reduction Strategy Paper Coverage in Southern Africa (December 2006)							
Country	I-PRSP Compl-etion[a]	PRSP Compl-etion[a]	First progress report[a]	Second progress report[a]	Third progress report[a]	Second PRSP Compl-etion[a]	HIPC Country
Countries finished or finalizing PRSPs							
Tanzania	Mar-00	Oct-00	Nov-01	Mar-03	Apr-04	Jun-05	Yes
Mozambique	Feb-00	Apr-01	Feb-03	Mar-04	Jun-05	Mar-05	Yes
Zambia	Jul-00	Mar-02	Mar-04	Dec-04	n.a	n.a	Yes
Malawi	Aug-00	Apr-02	Aug-03	May-05	Jan-06	n.a	Yes
Lesotho	Dec-00	Apr-06	n.a	n.a	n.a	n.a	No
D.R.C.	Mar-02	-	n.a	n.a	n.a	n.a	Yes
Countries in initial stages of PRSP process							
Angola	The Government, assisted by UNDP, devised an interim strategy known as the Estratégia de Combate à Pobreza (ECP). It was approved by the cabinet in February 2004.						
Zimbabwe	The PRSP process has been stalled due to the current political situation in the country.						
Note: n.a. = not applicable; I-PRSP = Interim Poverty Reduction Strategy Paper. [a] Date as indicated on country document							

The Poverty Reduction Strategy initiative has, in the years since its introduction, tended to concentrate predominantly on countries that are characteristically at the poorer end of the range of aid-dependent African countries eligible for concessional lending.[99] This is indeed evident in the Southern African context. To date, five of the 14 countries in the sub-region have fully completed PRSPs, namely (in chronological order) Tanzania, Mozambique, Zambia, Malawi and Lesotho (Table 4). The Lesotho PRSP is currently awaiting approval by the Boards of the World Bank and IMF. Tanzania and Mozambique were part of the first wave of countries that adopted and finalized PRSPs, and in the former case the development of a second generation Poverty Reduction Strategy is well under way and a draft document was distributed for comment in August 2004. The Democratic Republic of Congo has completed an Interim PRSP (I-PRSP) and was scheduled to finalise its drafting process by late 2005. In addition, the Angolan cabinet approved an interim strategy (Estratégia de Combate à Pobreza, ECP) in early 2004 though it has yet to be formally submitted to the IMF and World Bank. Some discussion has taken place on the possibility of preparing a PRSP in Zimbabwe, but the current political situation has forestalled this from being developed.

Migration and Poverty

The relationship between poverty and migration in the region has been shown to be both long-standing and especially complex, involving the movement of skilled migrants, contract workers, other legal migrants, asylum seekers, undocumented migrants and small entrepreneurs.[100] Cross-border and domestic migration is not only on the rise in SADC, but increasingly forms part of household economic diversification in response to dynamic and often difficult economic conditions.

There remain substantive gaps in understanding regional migration patterns and the links to poverty and poverty reduction policy. Nonetheless, research undertaken by the Southern African Migration Project has indicated, inter alia, that migration constitutes a salient part of the regional economy. In consequence, poverty reduction strategies in the region need to accommodate migration dynamics, especially since migrants form a central component of household-level livelihoods and coping strategies.[101] Policies that factor in population mobility have a greater likelihood of enhancing well-being.[102]

Migration Issues and Poverty Diagnostics in PRSPs

Recognising the cross-cutting nature of the migration dynamic within SADC, PRSPs and related poverty reduction strategies will have to incorporate migration and its linkages to poverty reduction to be truly effective. Yet, based upon a preliminary examination of those countries in Southern Africa that have produced I-PRSPs or full PRSPs, migration remains a notable omission. The PRSP is supposed to present a comprehensive diagnostic or profile that captures the determinants of poverty as a basis for informing the development of an appropriate programme of action. Virtually none of the reviewed documents from Southern Africa provide a detailed analysis of the relationship between poverty and migration in the national context. Of the six Southern

African states with either an interim or full PRSP, migration issues are practically absent in Tanzania and Zambia, though some reference is made in the poverty profiles contained in the Mozambique, Malawi and Lesotho PRSPs. The documentation from DRC and Angola remains exceptional relative to the other countries, since the reintegration and resettlement of refugees, displaced persons and ex-combatants remain central in a post-conflict situation. Other apparent tendencies among those countries mentioning migration is not to provide analysis of the purposes and outcomes of migration and to present a predominantly negative view of the effects of migration.

Tanzania

In Tanzania, one of the earliest adopters of the PRSP approach, the only discussion of migration issues in the poverty diagnostics section of the first full strategy document produced in October 2000 was the inclusion of refugees as one of the vulnerable groups that require social safety nets. However, in the draft version of the second PRSP released in August 2004, refugees had fallen off the list of vulnerable groups. This was apparently informed by a participatory poverty appraisal conducted during 2002.

Zambia

In the Zambian PRSP no mention is made of migration at all in relation to the discussion of poverty in the country. This is somewhat surprising given the intimate relationship that exists between migration and urban and rural poverty in the country. As one study observes:

> Rural households receive remittances from urban relatives, or send members to perform temporary migrant labour in cities, which absorb excess workers from heavily populated rural areas. The latter also provide a fall back option when urban workers are retrenched and fail to cope with the demands of urban life.[103]

However, there is some preliminary evidence to suggest that with the decline in the copper industry, urban unemployment and the attendant pressure placed upon remitted income, the significance of these coping strategies may have been eroded. For instance, the 2002-03 Living Conditions Monitoring study shows that remittances only accounted for 6% of household incomes in rural areas, with little variance across the income distribution.[104] Moreover, another study found that migration to urban areas was rarely mentioned as a coping mechanism during discussions of poverty, destitution and crop failure and there were indications that migration is now primarily from urban to rural areas, with some seasonal rural-rural movement to escape drought conditions.[105] This is corroborated by the results of the 2000 Census, which found that for the first time in three decades the share of the urban population had declined, from 40% in 1990 to 36% in 2000.[106] Household surveys suggest an even more pronounced migration trend than the census, with the urban share of the population falling from 46% in 1991 to 38% in 1998, with urban out-migration pronounced in the Copperbelt province.[107] The receipt of remittances from urban relatives is an oft-cited factor distinguishing the destitute from the less poor.[108] Nonetheless, fewer households were receiving remittances compared with five years earlier, due to the increasing inability of urban residents to fulfil extended family obligations as a result of mounting urban poverty and unemployment.

Malawi

Malawi's PRSP largely ascribes the poverty situation in the South region to in-migration, sees 'illegal immigration' as fuelling crime and limiting employment opportunities for Malawians and views labour migration as a contributing factor in the breakdown of male and female relations, increasing the likelihood of multiple or casual sexual partners and risk of HIV infection. What is not reflected in the strategy document is the increasing dependence of rural households on migration as a livelihoods strategy and as a means of survival during periods of hardship. Three types of demographic movement are particularly common. These are seasonal, internal rural migration in search of piecework (*ganyu*), permanent and seasonal migration to urban areas to gain additional income and, finally, cross-border into Mozambique, typically involving *ganyu* labour.[109]

During the 1990s, earnings from agricultural exports and remittances took a downturn, with adverse repercussions for most rural households. Remittances earned from male labour migration to South African mines continued a decline that began in the 1970s, while the opportunities for wage employment in the country's plantations shrunk because of declining global agricultural commodity prices and adverse economic trends.[110] The increasing difficulty encountered in securing rural liveli-hoods prompted individuals to move to urban centres, resulting in a dramatic process of urbanisation.[111] Migration flows accelerated during the 2001-2003 food crisis, with all three types of demographic move-ment increasing. In particular, there was a noticeable influx of people, predominantly women and children, to urban centres to search for casual labour or to beg.

Mozambique

Mozambique's Action Plan for the Reduction of Absolute Poverty (PARPA) simply alludes to internal migration as a cause of urban pov-erty and as potentially placing pressure on the non-agricultural job market. In addition, displacement attributable to the country's civil war is identified as a contributory factor to poverty and to growth and development dynamics in Maputo. The virtual absence of migration issues appears to have historical antecedents. For instance, population movement and the role of rural-rural labour migration in rural liveli-hoods and coping strategies was neglected in earlier key poverty-related documents produced by the Government of Mozambique.[112] This is in spite of evidence of high levels of population mobility in rural parts of the country, especially following the end of the civil war, as well as long-established migration patterns between Mozambique and its neighbours. Where official documents such as *Poverty Reduction Strategy for Mozambique* and *Mozambique: Rural Poverty Profile* do actually men-tion migration, they tend to exclusively emphasise the negative effects that rural out-migration has, such as increased dependency ratios and reduced labour availability.[113]

Lesotho

In Lesotho's PRSP, migration features quite prominently in relation to discussion of the changing nature of livelihood and poverty trends in the country over the past two decades. Migrant labour to the South African gold mines is described as having been the most secure form of income for generations. Nonetheless, the reduction in mineworker remittances due to retrenchments in South African mines during the 1990s is cited as one of the explanatory factors underlying the increas-ing number of poor Basotho households. This featured prominently in the community consultations that were conducted as part of the PRSP formulation process. The attrition in mine employment has provoked a transformation in the economic base of the country. The main driver of economic growth in Lesotho today is the export-orientated garment industry, and the country became Africa's largest exporter of textiles and apparel to the United States under the African Growth and Opportunity Act (AGOA).[114]

New, predominantly female employment opportunities were created in the garment industry, with more than 10,000 jobs created in 2001 alone and 19 garment factories opening in 2001-02, although some have since closed down again. The Lesotho PRSP raises concerns about the excess supply of migrant employment seekers and the consequent decline in the provision of services in urban areas as well as quality of life that this influx has begun to produce. This resonates in other literature that has expressed concern about low wages, the health costs associated with long hours spent working in factories, the high cost and poor quality of urban accommodation, household stress and disruption due to the new pattern of predominantly female internal migration, as well as the rise of social pathologies in urban areas.[115]

Angola and DRC

The PRSP processes in Angola and the DRC are distinct from those in other countries in the sub-region. Although such conflict-affected countries may share similar economic, governance and livelihoods challenges compared to other low-income African countries, they have the added challenge of addressing the specific forms of vulnerability and poverty that are often created during conflict.[116] This unfortunate legacy carries significant costs, including the destruction of physical infrastructure, loss of institutional and social capital, and flight of financial and human capital

Because of the particular challenges of resettlement, reintegration and reconstruction in the aftermath of conflict, it could be argued that PRSP-related documents produced in such contexts might be expected to be more inclined to discuss migration-related issues. The evidence from the DRC's I-PRSP and Angola's ECP tends to support this assertion. In the former instance, a recurrent theme is the incalculable economic, social, political and environmental cost of the civil war, especially for the estimated 4 million displaced citizens. The document highlights the immiserating effect that the war in the DRC had on both the displaced population and host communities. More specifically, prolonged displacement is identified as having been a determinant of pervasive malnutrition due to the disruption of livelihoods and market access, as well as a catalysing force behind the increasing urban face of poverty due to the predominantly urban-ward migration flows, and intense environmental pressure that these flows caused. The movement of armed combatants is also linked to increased gender-based violence and the transmission of disease.

The Angolan ECP emphasises emergency actions directed towards national reconstruction, and the social and economic reintegration of demobilised soldiers, the displaced and refugees into society. The document acknowledges that the protracted armed conflict in the country since independence has negatively impacted upon the free movement of people by triggering accelerated rural-urban and cross-border migration flows, and displacing an estimated four million Angolans, or a third of the population. The ECP goes on to discuss some of the effects of these involuntary migration processes. These include the impoverishment of the displaced population, with livelihoods strategies and coping mechanisms of families being disrupted. In turn, food insecurity and malnutrition escalated amongst the internally displaced and refugees. Pressure on urban infrastructure intensified, while the influx of unskilled labour into urban centres provoked a rapid expansion of the informal sector and placed upward pressure on unemployment. In common with the DRC's IPRSP, the Angolan ECP raises concerns about the potential spread of HIV/AIDS due to the removal of barriers to free movement following the cessation of hostilities and the transition to peace.

Policy and Programmatic Responses

Having found rather limited and somewhat uneven coverage of migration issues in the poverty diagnostics components of the PRSPs in Southern Africa, it would be expected that actual strategies to reduce poverty through migration policy would be similarly lacking. Indeed, this is the case. While migration-related concerns are raised (to varying degrees), virtually none of the PRSPs offer specific policy responses to migration.

Tanzania's first PRSP does not contain any specific policy recommendations that make explicit reference to migration.[117] In the draft version of the country's second PRSP, migration is referred to once in relation to housing delivery.[118] Similarly, Mozambique's PARPA hardly refers to migration in articulating its fundamental policy interventions.[119] Zambia's PRSP is not much better, with migration discussed within sections on HIV/AIDS and transport and infrastructure policy.[120] In contrast, the Malawian Poverty Reduction Strategy makes reference to migration in each of its four strategic pillars, which focus on strategies for enhancing sustainable pro-poor economic growth, human capital development, improving the quality of life of the most vulnerable, and good governance.[121] It is also referred to in the section on HIV/AIDS. Finally, in the case of Lesotho's recently completed PRSP, migration again features in a number of policy domains.[122] These include the cross-cutting themes of HIV/AIDS, the environment, and governance, in addition to health and rural and urban poverty. This is probably influenced by the central role that international labour migration played in rurally-based livelihood patterns in Lesotho until the early 1990s. With reduced South African mine labour opportunities, the nature of migration has changed, though its centrality to the livelihood of the population remains undiminished.[123]

The remainder of this section will examine in more detail the scope and nature of migration issues featured in the policy and programmatic interventions proposed by the five countries with full PRSPs (Tanzania, Mozambique, Zambia, Malawi and Lesotho). The analysis is grouped according to five thematic clusters of policy actions: (a) cross-cutting issues; (b) macro and structural issues; (c) rural and urban poverty; (d) human development; and (e) private sector and infrastructure. This will be followed by a similar analysis in relation to the PRSP documentation of the two conflict-affected countries in the region; Angola and the DRC.

Strategies Pertaining to Cross-cutting Issues

HIV/AIDS

Three PRSPs refer to the relationship between migration patterns and HIV/AIDS. Under the health and HIV/AIDS sections of Zambia's PRSP, refugees from neighbouring states are identified as a high-risk group for the transmission of HIV/AIDS and considered a "threat in some districts" since "an influx can have a significant impact on the resources available and the demands generated" for health and AIDS-related services.[124] To reduce the number of new HIV infections, the strategy document advocates a scaling-up of programmes aimed at promoting safe sex practices among high-risk groups, including refugees. The Malawi Poverty Reduction Strategy, while recognising that labour migration represents a notable livelihood strategy among the poor, goes on to associate it with the breakdown of male-female relations, which increases the likelihood of multiple or causal sexual partners and the risk of HIV infection.[125]

Lesotho's PRSP identifies migrants as a vulnerable group with a high-risk of HIV infection. In a concluding chapter on the risks that will be encountered during PRSP implementation, out-migration to South Africa is described as a phenomenon that will exacerbate the impact of HIV/AIDS as both result in the loss of productive members of the labour force and present a risk to economic growth. However, a study of migrant miners and their wives found that such concerns about the loss of productive labour due to out-migration appear unfounded.[126]

Governance and Poverty Reduction

In the context of governance strategies, migration tends to be considered in relation to the provision of security from corruption, crime, and violence. Malawi's PRSP tends to express rather strong sentiments, with increases in irregular migration in the country blamed for rising crime rates, reductions in economic opportunities for Malawian citizens and for undermining the integrity of Malawian passports.[127] In response, increasing the police presence in rural and border areas is proposed as a crime-reduction measure.

In the Lesotho PRSP, strengthening crime prevention and reducing the existing high crime rate have been designated as high priorities. This emphasis derives from the importance placed on security by communities all over Lesotho during community consultations. The document indicates that the Government of Lesotho will undertake specific, measurable activities to reduce cross-border crime, by sensitising communities along both sides of the border about cross-border crime and stock theft.

The commitment to addressing cross-border crime is an important step towards acknowledging the stock theft crisis in the country. Over the last decade, stock raiding has become a dangerous and pervasive form of two-way cross-border movement, coordinated by well-organised gangs in Lesotho and South Africa.[128] The increased incidence of stock theft has been attributed to growing joblessness and poverty, especially amongst the youth in the mountain areas of Lesotho. Ironically though, stock theft has deepened poverty by wiping out many rural livelihoods, increasing the risk attached to livestock ownership, reducing wool and mohair production, disrupting communal cooperation such as livestock loaning and threatening the livelihoods and personal security of herdboys and their dependents. It has also fostered counter-raids to retrieve lost stock, revenge attacks and vigilantism.[129] The lingering question is whether the proposed process of sensitisation is sufficient to resolve the crisis.

Apart from strategies for reducing cross-border crime, the Lesotho PRSP also draws a relationship between migrant labour and increasing domestic violence against women. The document describes how male migrants may turn violent when they discover that their partners have been unfaithful in their absence, or as a result of feeling powerless following entrenchment from the mines.

Environment

In the Lesotho PRSP, concerns are raised about the environmental cost of rapid in-migration to Maseru and Maputsoe due to processes of industrialisation. These include the environmental health risks that may result from the overburdening of municipal waste management capacity, together with poor waste disposal practices.

Gender and Empowerment

With regard to gender issues, the Malawi PRSP discusses how the low education levels of women relative to men may have affected their access to formal employment and other economic resources. Male migration to towns and estates in search of paid employment is viewed as having compounded this situation, with women who have low rates of literacy being left behind to manage the farms and families.

Rural and Urban Poverty Strategies

Recognising the salient role that migrant remittances have played in subsidising food crop production, the Lesotho PRSP argues that the mine retrenchments of the 1990s have adversely affected food security. Prospects for sharecropping have also diminished due to increased unemployment, placing further strain on household food security.[130] Lesotho's PRSP also identifies immigration as a priority for poverty reduction. The emphasis is on improving the application and issuing of passports, visas and working permits, and tracking 'illegal immigrants,' since they are perceived as potential tax evaders, and as a source of competition for scarce employment opportunities.

In Tanzania's draft second PRSP, migration is referred to once in the section on 'Improved sanitation and shelter in urban and rural areas' and in relation to housing delivery.[131] More specifically, it is mentioned that the government's rate of provision of houses in urban areas is being outpaced by rural-urban migration. In stating this, slow housing delivery in urbanising areas is not being explained as a shortcoming of government's response to the need for adequate shelter. Rather, blame is transferred to migrants themselves.

Human Development Strategies

Health

Only two PRSPs (Malawi and Lesotho) have health care strategies that accommodate migration issues. In the Malawi document, the country's poor health indicators are attributed to the shortage of qualified medical personnel, especially in rural areas. Internal and international migration in the health sector due to low remuneration and poor career prospects are mentioned as exacerbating the situation.[132] In improving the quality of essential healthcare, the Government of Malawi has committed itself to reviewing the remuneration and career structures for medical staff to address problems of attrition through 'brain drain.' Lesotho's PRSP also acknowledges the contribution of health personnel with regard to the quality of and access to health care services, especially in combating HIV/AIDS.[133] It further recognises the need for the government to provide necessary support, and prioritises the reviewing and improving of the working conditions of health personnel as a means of addressing the high rate of staff turnover and brain drain.[134]

Social Protection

The link between migration and social protection is twofold. Firstly, through the transfer of remittances, migration may act as a social protection strategy to reduce the risk of shocks that occur or to help cope with shocks once they have happened. Second, migration may create new needs for social protection measures amongst those who are left behind.[135] However, an appreciation of this relationship is not evident in the Southern African PRSP documents, with migration analysis missing from discussion of social protection and safety net interventions. The main exception is the Malawi PRSP. In a section on social protection for the chronically poor and vulnerable, direct welfare support interventions are advocated for individuals (especially orphans) who are forced to move to urban centres and beg in unhealthy conditions, due to over-stretched informal safety nets.[136] Even in this case, the role of migrants as agents of development is overlooked, focusing instead only on the demand side of social protection.

Private Sector and Infrastructure Strategies

Transport

A recurrent theme in three PRSPs in the region (Mozambique, Zambia and Malawi) is the integral role of transport in the livelihood strategies of the poor, and how a lack of mobility can detrimentally affect income, health, and vulnerability.[137] The provision of basic access roads together with effective and affordable transport services can facilitate access to markets, employment opportunities and social services, promote social contact between migrants and the families they leave behind, as well as reduce the impacts of household-level risks. It is therefore important that transportation infrastructure should form an essential element of poverty reduction strategies.

In expanding opportunities for the poor, Mozambique's PRSP views the development of basic infrastructure as a fundamental role of the state.[138] Infrastructure, in particular improvements in road networks, is seen as playing a contributory role in enabling better access to markets and facilitating mobility, especially for those who live in rural areas and depend on agriculture. The Zambian PRSP raises concerns about the poor state of rural feeder roads and the extent to which this inhibits mobility and accessibility, thus deepening poverty in rural areas.[139] In an attempt to improve mobility in rural areas, expansion, rehabilitation and investment in the road sector is advocated, together with measures aimed at facilitating the introduction and promotion of appropriate motorised and non-motorised modes of transport. Finally, the Malawi PRSP aims to improve rural infrastructure by investing in rural roads.[140] It is expected that this will have a direct impact on linking rural, urban and peri-urban areas, with gains in accessibility subsequently reducing transport costs and creating marketing opportunities. Rural feeder roads also have social benefits through better access to social services by facilitating mobility.

Displacement and Poverty Reduction Strategies in Angola and the DRC

A strong feature of the strategy content in the two conflict affected countries was the inclusion of policies and interventions focused on addressing the devastating consequences of conflict. More specifically, they appear to be displacement-sensitive in that the situation and needs of returnees and internally-displaced persons are explicitly considered in formulating the policy action programmes. This conforms with a recent study of PRSPs in conflict-affected countries which found that countries recently out of war tend to devote most attention to policy actions that deal with the consequences of violent conflict.[141]

In Angola, proposed actions revolve predominantly around the reintegration of *deslocados* (internally displaced persons), refugees, demobilised Unita soldiers and their dependent families.[142] Social reinsertion thus appears as the priority intervention area of the strategy and is being addressed through the government's Post Conflict Social Reintegration Strategy, together with the legislative framework and institutional structures that have been established to strengthen the process. This programme entails proposals aimed at facilitating the movement of these people to their areas of origin or resettlement areas, as well as supporting their reintegration through the promotion of productive activities and the provision of basic social services. Displaced populations are also explicitly targeted in the proposed interventions in a number of other sector priority areas. These include a food security and rural development programme aimed at developing the agricultural sector and satisfying food needs, a health sector programme to address the concern about a potential rise in HIV/AIDS with increased migratory patterns, an adult literacy programme, an employment creation programme, a housing programme, and projects that deal with mine clearance and improving road networks to encourage the movement of people and goods.

A similar, though more circumscribed, focus permeates the DRC's I-PRSP, putting a strong emphasis on demobilisation and reintegration under the pillar of peace and good governance.[143] To address poverty and its exacerbation by conflict, the I-PRSP proposes a post-conflict reconstruction and economic recovery programme. Firstly, the demobilisation component of this intended programme recognises that reuniting families, resettling displaced communities and refugees, and continuing the demobilization and reintegration of child soldiers is instrumental to achieving lasting peace. Secondly, in relation to reintegration, the programme proposes to address the needs of the victims of the fighting with a suite of interventions that incorporate psychological, socioeconomic and medical rehabilitation, education and vocational training, health, housing and the reconstruction of basic infrastructure (transport, communication, energy, roads, rail and waterways network).

A recent review of PRSP processes in conflict-affected societies expresses concern at the relative "lack of analysis of the key tensions remaining within society and policy actions, as well as trade-offs required to reduce these and prevent future conflict."[144] While this may be true of the DRC's IPRSP, some of the subsequent documentation is beginning to acknowledge residual tensions.[145] For instance, the second PRSP Preparation Status Report outlines various risks that could compromise the quality and timely completion of the PRSP.[146] These include resurging violence, a lack of coherence, pre-electoral political pressures and weak administrative capacity. A resurgence of violence in the east would effectively block the participatory process in that region. Also, the PRSP process could be derailed if political pressures cause the authorities to compromise their hitherto effective coordination of economic and financial policies. Although progress has continued toward reunification of the country, tensions in the east have increased, with fighting in a number of cities. Such tensions, which so far have been

successfully dealt with, may recur and test the strength of the government's unity and the support of the international community, as well
as the good faith of neighbouring countries.

Apart from Angola and the DRC, which accounted for the world's
highest return movements in 2004, it is important to briefly mention
the treatment of displacement issues in the PRSPs of refugee-hosting
countries.[147] At the end of 2003, Tanzania was host to an estimated
650,000 refugees, predominantly from Burundi and the DRC, while
Zambia hosted approximately 227,000 refugees, mostly from Angola
and the DRC.[148] In both cases, the refugees have been in the country
for extended periods of time, in some cases for more than 20 years.
The PRSP documents of these host countries only sporadically refer to
refugees (if at all), and tend to emphasise the negative effects of hosting
them. In Tanzania's first PRSP the only mention of refugees is in relation to the growing numbers of refugees that many communities have
to deal with (together with burgeoning populations of AIDS victims
and orphans, the handicapped and the aged) and the consequent need
for safety-nets.[149] No mention of such displacement issues is incorporated into the second PRSP.[150] In Zambia, the influx of refugees into
certain districts is discussed in relation to increasing both the pressure
on available local resources and the demand for health care services.
Even the DRC itself, which hosted Burundian and Rwandan refugees
in the eastern part of the country in 1994, referred in its I-PRSP to the
environmental degradation that this produced, characterised by "deforestation and the destruction of fauna in the wildlife parks."[151]

Migration Content of Documentation Guiding PRSPs

PRSPs in Southern Africa tend to underemphasise migration and treat
it as a negative phenomenon. Does this neglect reflect an inherent
gap or flaw in the PRSP approach itself or, alternatively, is it symptomatic of factors such as negative government attitudes and imperfect
information on migration patterns at the country level? This section
endeavours to answer these questions and stimulate further dialogue
and critical debate.

Although country teams were afforded substantive autonomy in
the process of designing their PRSPs, guidance on poverty-related
measurement, analysis and policy was provided through at least three

significant World Bank/IMF documents. These are the *Poverty Reduction Strategy Papers—Operational Issues*, intended to provide general directions on the development of the PRSPs, together with the World Bank's *Poverty Reduction Strategy Papers: Internal Guidance Note* (1999) and the *Poverty Reduction Strategy Paper Sourcebook* (World Bank, 2001).[152] It is therefore useful to preface the migration audit of PRSPs with a cursory examination of the extent and nature of migration analysis in these instructive texts. This would provide some indication as to whether national poverty reduction strategies are consistent or incongruous with the views expressed in these documents.

The first two documents contain no migration analysis or even pointers as to where national teams might consider focusing on mobile populations. Nonetheless, the PRSP Sourcebook addresses migration in a number of its 23 chapters. The Sourcebook is divided into three broad thematic sections: core techniques (6 chapters), cross-cutting issues (5 chapters) and macro and sectoral issues (12 chapters). It is in the latter that most of the references to migration are to be found, especially in the chapters on rural and urban poverty.

With regard to the chapter on rural poverty, it is important to distinguish between the version contained in the draft PRSP Sourcebook and the final published version, as the extent to which migration issues are incorporated varies enormously. In the draft version of the chapter, the treatment of migration issues is fairly balanced, reflecting the inherent complexity of contemporary migration dynamics. On the positive side, the relationship between the roles of migration and remittances in reducing deprivation in rural localities is emphasised. Rural out-migration is recognised as affecting both migrants and those remaining behind and is regarded as an important strategy by which members of low income households can escape poverty.[153] Labour migration, whether seasonal or permanent, is acknowledged as playing "a critical role in shaping the livelihoods of poor households in developing countries" while in the long term, "rural-urban migration is an integral part of the process of structural change and a powerful mechanism for reducing rural poverty."[154] This view of migration is qualified with a statement indicating that the migratory process may impose "external costs on urban residents in the form of greater congestion (for living and travelling), increased pollution and lower quality of life (larger classes in public schools lead to lowering of educational quality)."[155] Remittances are viewed as an important corollary of migration, particularly for family members who remain in the migrant's area of origin, contributing towards the diversification of household income in the face of risk and providing a means of investing in household assets. The draft chapter goes on to propose questions that PRSP architects should engage with in respect to migration and remittances.

In relation to the development of policy, the draft Sourcebook chapter suggests that national PRSP teams accept unrestricted population movement as the norm and focus on including policies that "enable the rural poor to benefit from migration."[156] The removal of formal barriers to migration is seen as an appropriate pro-poor measure since policies that restrict migration have an adverse impact on the rural poor. However, while advocating the removal of such barriers, there is a parallel recognition that "systems for facilitating and monitoring the flow of migrant populations in destination areas may be needed."[157] At the sectoral level, mention is made of improving transport and communication infrastructure to facilitate temporary labour migration in search of off-farm employment, as well as the movement of agricultural produce to markets.[158] The chapter also recognises that migration is selective and that for rural households that contain few economically active members and a high dependency ratio, public transfers may constitute the only realistic pathway out of poverty.

While this provides a useful set of guidelines that could assist in mainstreaming migration into the various sections of the poverty reduction strategies, much of this content was lost in the published version of the Sourcebook.[159] This is highly regrettable and future editions of the Sourcebook should re-incorporate this material.

The urban poverty chapter promotes an equally positive view of migration. This is evident in the attempt to dispel certain preconceptions surrounding rural-urban migration, notably internal migration as a cause of urban poverty. On the one hand, urban poverty can partially be a reflection of active rural-urban migration, as cities provide better opportunities to improve individual welfare.[160] Nonetheless, research on internal migration has indicated that "migrants are not necessarily among the poorest members of their original or receiving communities."[161] In addition, rural-urban migration accounts for less than half of urban growth, with natural population increases within cities and the incorporation of former rural areas at the urban periphery the most significant sources of growth. Therefore, given that migration is not a major cause of urban poverty, the chapter stresses that controlling migration should not be considered an appropriate policy response,

as it hurts the poor and the overall labour market, and is usually ineffectual in curbing poverty rates.[162] Ensuring that the potential gains
from rural-urban migration are progressively realised is contingent on
the ability of cities and towns to manage growth, provide good governance, and ensure services for households and small enterprises. Efficient
urban development is recognised as playing a major role in addressing
national poverty.[163]

With regard to public actions to address urban poverty, several broad
areas of intervention are recommended. These include increasing access
to employment opportunities for surplus rural labour migrating to cities, as well as managing the additional demand imposed by rural-urban
migrants on city infrastructure by measures relating to tenure security,
property rights and land and infrastructure regulations. Other areas
include public finance (cost recovery, tariffs and subsidies) and urban
governance (public accountability and responsiveness, anti-corruption
policies and capacity building), though these do not explicitly focus on
internal migration.

Other sectoral policy areas in the PRSP Sourcebook where migration
is discussed include education, social protection, transport and mining.
Education is regarded as being a powerful instrument for reducing deprivation and vulnerability. More specifically, education is discussed as a
catalyst for, amongst other things, expanding labour mobility and raising earnings potential.[164] The migration of teachers to more attractive
employment is also mentioned as a factor complicating the capacity of
African countries to produce an adequate teacher supply.[165] The social
protection chapter indicates that previous interventions have failed to
target refugees and internally displaced persons, which are groups that
may be "highly correlated with poverty but outside the reach of traditional mechanisms and sympathies."[166] The transport chapter identifies
high transport costs as a barrier to mobility, thus making it difficult
for rural households to maintain social contacts in the city, and for
migrants to remain close to the families left behind.[167] The transport
sector is further recognized as having a key role in HIV/AIDS prevention, and argues that interventions should be specifically targeted at
transport institutions and workers such as long-haul truckers.[168] As for
mining, the Sourcebook discusses migration in relation to its health
and socio-cultural impacts. Due to the dislocated family context of
many migrant mineworkers, they are seen as being at high risk of HIV/
AIDS and other communicable diseases. They are also seen as especially susceptible to work-related injuries, which places them and their

families in particularly precarious situations.[169] Mining projects are also highlighted as a potential risk to sociocultural stability, as the lure of new opportunities creates in-migration, which may provoke tensions between 'original residents' and 'newcomers.'[170]

Finally, attention is devoted to migration as part of the cross-cutting chapter on gender.[171] Reference is made to:

- The need to incorporate a gender focus into poverty analysis in the PRSPs, in part by examining access to labour markets, constraints on mobility and the consequences of migration decisions in responses to rapid economic and social change;

- The growth of female-headed households due to migration (amongst other reasons), which means that the insecurity women face in the labour market directly affects children and other dependents.

From the analysis presented in this section, it is apparent that the PRSP Sourcebook provides reasonably detailed guidance as to how country-level development officials might go about producing a migration-sensitive poverty reduction strategy. While some of Southern Africa's PRSPs predate the publication of the draft and final versions of the Sourcebook (Tanzania, Mozambique), the extent to which migration analysis has been integrated into the more recent strategies (Malawi, Zambia, Lesotho) is disappointing.

Chapter

4 POVERTY REDUCTION STRATEGIES IN MIDDLE-INCOME COUNTRIES

Migration and Poverty Reduction Strategies in non-PRSP Countries

The remaining six SADC countries (Botswana, Namibia, South Africa, Swaziland, Seychelles and Mauritius) are not eligible for World Bank/IMF supported Poverty Reduction Strategies due to their middle-income status. Nonetheless, a number of these countries have independently produced national poverty reduction strategies (Table 5). Botswana's National Strategy for Poverty Reduction has been formulated but has not yet been implemented, whereas the Mauritian National Action Plan for Poverty Alleviation is currently being implemented.[172] Namibia produced a Poverty Reduction Strategy, National Poverty Reduction Action Programme and National Development Plan.[173] South Africa has introduced many PRSP-type reforms, moving from broad strategies on poverty reduction as articulated in the Reconstruction and Development Programme (RDP) towards sector specific programmes governed by the Growth, Employment and Redistribution macroeconomic strategy.[174] Finally, in Swaziland, the Poverty Reduction Unit, based in the Ministry of Economic Planning and Development, is finalising its Poverty Reduction Strategy and Action Plan (PRSAP), with a draft version released in the public domain in December 2005.[175]

Table 5: Poverty Reduction Strategies in Middle Income Countries in Southern Africa			
Country	Economic classification	Title of Poverty Strategy	PRS Completion
Countries not eligible for PRSPs			
Botswana	UMC	National Strategy for Poverty Reduction (NSPR);	2003
		National Development Plan 9 (NDP9, 2003-2009)	2003
Namibia	LMC	Poverty Reduction Strategy;	1998
		National Poverty Reduction Action Programme (NPRAP);	2001
		National Development Plan (NDP2)	2002
Mauritius	UMC	Mauritian National Action Plan for Poverty Alleviation (APPA)	2001
Seychelles	UMC	n.a.	
South Africa	LMC	Reconstruction and Development Programme;	1994
		Growth, Employment and Redistribution (GEAR);	1996
		Provincial Growth and Development Strategies;	Various dates
		Municipal-level Integrated Development Plans	Various dates
Swaziland	LMC	Reduction Strategy and Action Plan (PRSAP)	Being finalized
Note: LMC = lower middle income country; UMC = upper middle income country.			

Unfortunately, an analysis of the sensitivity to migration of poverty reduction strategies in middle income countries in the Southern African region is constrained by the limited public availability of many of the aforementioned documents. The Botswana NSPR and Mauritian APPA, although published a couple of years ago, are not readily accessible. The focus here is therefore on South Africa, Namibia and Swaziland.

South Africa: National Development Strategies

Since the transition to democracy in 1994, the South African government has demonstrated a resolute commitment to addressing poverty and inequality. Not only has the state introduced an impressive range of anti-poverty initiatives, but there has been an equally impressive commitment in terms of resource allocations for these measures. Yet, in spite of this resolve, there is a need for greater focus and coherence in the country's poverty reduction strategy.[176] This section will focus on a selection of poverty-focused development strategies that have been instituted since 1994 at the national, provincial and local government levels.

The Reconstruction and Development Programme (1994)

The Reconstruction and Development Programme (RDP) was initially formulated as the 1994 ANC election manifesto.[177] With the subsequent publication of the RDP White Paper, which set the broad framework for economic and social policy, it became the core development policy document of the first post-apartheid government.[178] While the RDP Base Document reflected a strong concern for the historical legacy of poor spatial planning, it was rather vague in addressing processes of urbanisation.[179]

Most of the discussion about migration in the RDP Base Document can be broadly categorized into several overarching themes. The first of these was the manner in which policies that were designed to ensure a migratory labour supply to the mines and the ethnic division of South Africa under the apartheid system produced spatial dislocation and fragmentation. The document described how entire communities were placed in localities where their economic viability was (and remains) extremely tenuous, resulting in pronounced geographic disparities.[180] It also lamented how, under apartheid, poor South Africans were moved "away from job opportunities and access to amenities", which "burdened the workforce with enormous travel distances to their places of employment and commercial centres, and thus with excessive costs."[181] Reference was also made to the disempowering effects of labour migration, both for workers and their families.[182] Recognising that migrant labour is going to remain an enduring feature of South Africa's economy and a salient livelihood strategy, the RDP base document contained proposals on the development of a suite of housing types to cater for the differential needs of migrant workers and those engaged in circular migration.[183]

The second migration-related theme evident in the RDP relates to urbanisation and urban development. The document cautioned on the need to consider the consequences of macroeconomic policies on the spatial distribution of economic activity. It also drew attention to the need for strategies "to address the excessive growth of the largest urban centres, the skewed distribution of population within rural areas, the role of small and medium-sized towns, the future of declining towns and regions, and the apartheid dumping grounds."[184] Taking cognisance of the fact that the majority of the country's gross domestic product (GDP) and population is concentrated in urban areas, the RDP acknowledged that "even with a strong rural development effort, economic activities will remain concentrated in the cities."[185] In response, the development of a comprehensive national urban strategy was advocated in order to "help serve the cities' rapidly growing populations and address the inequities and structural imbalances caused by the apartheid system."[186] Therefore, while vague in detail, the RDP did appear to adopt a more balanced view of urbanisation, as suggested by proposals aimed at long-term, sustainable urban development while simultaneously promoting growth and equity.

The final theme relates to cross-border migration to South Africa. Based upon an understanding that efforts aimed at reconstruction and the building of the domestic economy could not occur in isolation from its Southern African neighbours, the RDP stressed the importance of regional cooperation, coordination and integration. At the heart of this proposal was a concern that alternative development trajectories would inhibit the growth and market potential of other countries in the sub-region, which would exacerbate the persistently high rates of unemployment and underemployment and promote increased migration to South Africa.[187] Here the RDP Base Document contained somewhat contradictory and inconsistent messages in relation to migration, calling for managed urbanisation on the one hand, while trying to discourage international migration to South Africa on the other.

The content of the RDP White Paper, introduced in November 1994, was not considered dissimilar to the RDP Base Document. However, it was more neoliberal in its outlook.[188] From a migration perspective, there is quite a significant departure from the Base Document. The only surviving direct reference to population mobility is in relation to the need for regional cooperation as a means of promoting stability and development.

The Growth, Employment and Redistribution Programme (1996)

In June 1996, the South African government adopted a five-year macroeconomic strategy entitled the Growth, Employment and Redistribution (GEAR) programme.[189] The emphasis of this strategy was on macroeconomic policy measures, which stressed the fairly orthodox combination of deficit reduction, tight monetary policy and trade liberalisation.[190] A number of microeconomic policy proposals were also contained in the GEAR document, though these have been criticised as poorly developed.[191] The document views poverty and inequality reduction as outcomes of employment creation, which in turn relies on private investment-led growth and increased labour market flexibility.[192] A secondary role is played by government investment in social and basic services for the poor.

The GEAR strategy effectively overlooked migration altogether. The only direct reference to be found is in the appendices to the document and in relation to the structural features of the South African labour market. It noted that apartheid-based labour migration had transformed into more complex rural-urban linkages, while the process of urbanisation had been slower than anticipated due to the slow rate of formal employment creation.[193] Due to a concern over the downward pressure that market liberalisation and global competition may exert on unskilled labour, the strategy went on to advocate measures to facilitate labour market flexibility for low-wage industries and create jobs for unskilled and semi-skilled work-seekers. The failure to represent migration in the GEAR strategy may be symptomatic of the prominent role assigned to traditional macroeconomic policy and the associated scaling back of government's role in addressing the post-apartheid development challenge. The content of the GEAR policy therefore visibly diverged from the RDP, with the latter not only defining a more proactive set of responsibilities for the state, but also affording comparably more consideration to the migration-development relationship in the formulation of policy.

Integrated Sustainable Rural Development and Urban Renewal Programmes (2000)

In his February 2001 State of the Nation address at the opening of Parliament, President Mbeki reaffirmed the government's commitment to addressing the needs of both the rural and urban poor, and announced the Urban Renewal Programme (URP) and the Integrated Strategic Rural Development Programme (ISRDP).[194] The principal aim of these programmes was "to conduct a sustained campaign against rural and urban poverty and underdevelopment, bringing in the resources of all three spheres of government – national, provincial and local – in a co-ordinated manner."[195] In addition, both aimed to encourage local innovation and creativity; promote interdepartmental and intergovernmental coordination to facilitate integrated service delivery; and pursue a decentralized, participatory and partnership-driven mode of development planning.[196]

Apart from their common aims, the two programmes share a number of basic design features. Foremost among these is the mutual reliance on a development node approach, with the ISRDP operating in 13 rural nodal points (mostly entire district municipalities) and the URP being implemented in eight urban nodes (former township areas). Corresponding to the government's concern about an incipient culture of dependency on state-provided welfare, there is a focus on creating productive employment for the poor rather than broader-based social protection measures. The programmes are also designed to align with municipal-level integrated development plans.[197] The responsibility for managing and coordinating the implementation of these programmes was assigned to the Department of Provincial and Local Government, with the assistance of the Independent Development Trust (IDT). Finally, they are both characterised by a phased approach, with implementation processes scheduled to run up until 2010.

From a migration perspective, the programmes are relatively weak. On the positive side, the policy documents do suggest the importance of considering rural-urban linkages in the pursuance of development and poverty reduction objectives. For instance, the ISRDP states that:

> Framing a successful rural development strategy will...depend on taking into account and understanding the diverse and complex realities that constitute the "rural areas." Besides the diversity of the rural areas, successful planning and implementation of rural development will require an understand-

ing of the complex linkages that exist between rural and urban areas.[198]

The document goes on to provide a typology of different forms of rural-urban linkage evident in the South African context. Nonetheless, it fails to carry this understanding of the interdependent and mobile nature of rural and urban lives and places into the design of suitable planning approaches and long-term programmatic vision and supportive measures.

Several studies have critically analysed the content and emerging outcomes of these two spatial programmes. They suggest that the programmes rest upon the notion of distinct 'rural' and 'urban' spaces. This signifies a notable disjuncture with current development thinking, in that they tend to overlook the multifaceted, interconnected character of people and places, and instead encourage a perception that these areas are competing and non-complimentary.[199] A second concern relates to the reductionism that pervades the programmes. The tendency to advocate interventions and investment in underdeveloped areas in the hope of tapping into latent potential to create productive spaces is fundamentally flawed. For instance, this belief tends to obscure the relative importance of migration and remittances as poverty-reducing strategies. Third, the overemphasis on rural space has, in the case of the ISRDP, resulted in the programme ultimately becoming "inherently anti-urban and bent on keeping the youth locked up in rural places."[200] Fourthly, the fixation of the programme on agrarian-led land reform as the means to a rural renaissance is inappropriate, especially as a strategy for preventing the youth from leaving rural areas.[201] Finally, the URP's focus on select nodal points in urban areas "concentrates on improving the lives of people in selected parts of the city only", which may ultimately divert attention from the broader policy concern of confronting the fragmentation of the apartheid city and the associated need for city-wide regeneration.[202]

National Spatial Development Perspective (2003)

The National Spatial Development Perspective (NSDP) has been hailed as "the first real spatial policy to emanate from the ANC government."[203] Noting that the spatial allocation of resources in South Africa has been occurring in an incoherent manner, the NSDP's spatial strategy assumes a differentiated approach that targets interventions to both places and people. As one commentator asserts, the NSDP is:

Steeped in the more recent understanding and appreciation of the need to strike the necessary fine balances between need and potential in the country, and calls for a nuanced approach to investing in the country: (1) Investing hard infrastructure in places with development potential so as to ensure that these places provide the maximum contribution to the national economy and the state fiscus; and (2) investing in people in places with limited potential so as to increase their market intelligence, increase their skills and give them more choice should they want to move to places with more development potential.[204]

Another asserts that the real contribution of the NSDP is the explicit argument for a specific kind of development approach in contrast to the rather nebulous, rhetorical policy statements that preceded it.[205] They caution against an uncritical adoption of the NSDP framework in making resource allocation decisions, as it may yield unintended consequences. These include the potential bias of planners in the complex process of deciphering "development potential"; the possible over-representation of urban areas amongst those areas identified as possessing high potential due to their comparative advantage in terms of skills and resources to lobby for investment; and the possible prioritization of areas with actual over latent potential.[206]

South Africa: Provincial Growth and Development Strategies

Since 1996, South Africa's provincial governments have formulated their own growth and development strategies. The Provincial Growth and Development Strategy (PGDS) has been developed as "a critical tool to guide and coordinate the allocation of national, provincial and local resources and private sector investment to achieve sustainable development outcomes."[207] Its primary purpose is "to provide a collaborative framework to drive implementation within a province."[208] Provincial governments are expected to assume a vital role in ensuring that economic planning, infrastructure investment and development expenditure is aligned with the approach and principles enshrined in the National Spatial Development Perspective. In short, this development framework has been conceptualized as the core strategic mechanism for effective, coordinated action to address the legacies of the apartheid space economy, promote sustainable growth and ensure poverty reduction and employment creation.[209]

Eastern Cape

The Eastern Cape's *Strategy Framework for Growth and Development 2004-2014* emphasises the deep structural poverty and spatial inequality that is the legacy of the province containing two former homelands (Transkei and Ciskei), which were 'established under apartheid as densely populated suppliers of migrant labour.'[210] The document refers explicitly to the challenge of addressing the lingering intra-provincial disparities between impoverished, densely populated labour reserves and comparatively affluent, sparsely populated commercial agricultural areas, and between well-serviced urban centres and under-serviced townships and informal settlements.[211] The significant contributory role of remittances as an income source in cash-constrained and employment deprived rural households is also documented.[212] The provincial strategy tends to mirror some of the shortcomings mentioned in relation to the ISRDP and URP, including the over-emphasis on rural areas, the cursory attention to migratory patterns, and the abundant faith in 'agrarian transformation', together with interventions in the tourism and manufacturing sectors.

Western Cape

The Western Cape's development profile identifies the seasonality in agricultural employment as a primary determinant of the sizable differences in the human development index values between urban and rural African and coloured population groups. The document lists in-migration from poorer provinces and rapid urbanisation as potential threats to the capacity for development, since it is perceived that these will further burden already inadequate metropolitan infrastructure, erode the economic base of the rural areas and bring about serious environmental degradation. In response, a rather dualistic message emerges; namely a strong desire to stem in-migration into the metropolitan area through targeted rural development interventions, while simultaneously acknowledging that the needs of those that do move to the city will need to be addressed. The following two extracts give a useful impression of the inconsistent and dualistic attitude towards migration in the province:

Unless the seasonal and undiversified economies of the Western Cape hinterland are redirected to provide scope for improved human conditions of the poor, people will migrate to the metropole to obtain the benefit of the better conditions there. The establishment of strategic safety nets to tide people over in times of temporary hardships such as droughts and seasonal unemployment, could also contribute towards containing irrational migration to the metropole - where real relief of poverty could be questionable. One also needs to attend to a balance in service provision to the hinterland and the metropole.[213]

A significant level of migration of people to the Province from the not so well endowed areas is likely to continue. In this regard there is a huge responsibility to accommodate them in a fashion that would not be to the detriment of the existing citizens...The provision of basic needs services to the new arrivals as well as their integration into the economy, is just as important.[214]

In terms of demography, mention is made of the rapid increase of migrants into the Cape Metropolitan area since the abolition of influx control in 1986, a large share of which are of Eastern Cape origin.[215] The profile also recognizes the development needs of those residing in sparsely populated communities to prevent further migration to the metropolitan area and development efforts aimed at the poor in the urban residential areas of the Cape Flats.[216]

Dualistic thinking spills over into the development vision, mission and objectives that are outlined for the province. The province's ability to create employment opportunities for in-migrants is lauded and, at the same time, the need to develop new resources to accommodate the infrastructural and human capacity requirements of in-migrants is recognized.[217] More explicitly, a primary objective of the Western Cape PGDS is to minimise "the urban and rural (core/periphery) divide through integrating urban and rural development and focusing more resources on neglected rural areas."[218] This is to be achieved by, amongst other things, "providing and maintaining other physical infrastructure to rural areas thus improving their attractiveness as areas to settle and work in."[219] The key development areas of the proposed strategy include the agriculture, tourism, manufacturing and transport sectors of the economy, together with human resource development and the

provision of basic needs (water, sanitation, health, housing, social services, and so on).

Gauteng

In Gauteng's PGDS, migration is viewed as a driver of a number of det-
rimental social phenomena. The province receives more migrants than
any other province, a development which has led to rapid economic
growth and expanded social service delivery.[220] This has triggered concerns about mounting unemployment, as job seekers are moving into
the province faster than the formal labour market can absorb them.[221]
Population growth and urbanisation are portrayed as significant environmental challenges, with references made to deteriorating air quality, habitat destruction/transformation and fragmentation and the loss
of biodiversity.[222] In combination, these challenges are seen as "an
increasing burden on Gauteng's stability and sustainability" and, if left
unchecked, "will pose a significant complication for the future prosper-
ity and development of the Province."[223] Virtually no direct mention is
made of migration in relation to the growth and development strategy.
The only apparent exceptions are (a) facilitating population mobility by
ensuring an accessible, affordable, reliable, integrated and environmen-
tally sustainable public transport system, and (b) making allowances for
in-migration in the determination of appropriate baseline development
targets.[224]

South Africa: Municipal Integrated Development Plans

The Integrated Development Plan (IDP) was introduced by legislation
in 1996 as a comprehensive and strategic approach to promoting local
development in South Africa. More specifically, it represents an instrument designed to provide strategic guidance to municipalities to link
and coordinate the many different sectoral plans and planning processes at the local government level. In its conception, the IDP was also
partially cast as a means of supporting more efficient financial and
resource allocation at the municipal level.[225] Between 1996 and 2000,
coinciding with a transitional phase of local government in the country,
a first round of IDPs was prepared by most local authorities. These first
efforts are generally considered to have been a disappointment. They
are viewed as poorly compiled documents containing analysis of low

quality, based on inadequate participatory processes and insufficiently linked to planning processes within other spheres of government.[226]

Following the local government elections of 2000 a second round of IDP formulation was undertaken, ushering in a gradual, ongoing process of refinement and maturation of the integrated development planning approach. Two events provided the basis for this round of IDPs; the passing of the Municipal Systems Act (2000), which made it a legislative requirement for municipalities to formulate an IDP and to review it on an annual basis to accommodate changing circumstances, and the second local government demarcation in 2000.[227] Early indications are that the practice of integrated development planning is facilitating rising levels of participation, greater support for IDPs and improvements in the quality of plans.[228] In accordance with the specifications of the Municipal Systems Act, most of the IDPs have a fairly uniform architecture. The content generally includes: a vision for long-term development; a situation analysis; development priorities; objectives and strategies; a spatial development framework; a set of sectoral plans; programmes and projects to be implemented over a five year period; financial and operational plans; and a framework for monitoring and evaluation.

In many respects, IDPs are premised upon a set of principles that are not dissimilar to those that inform the PRSP approach. They both place a singular emphasis on process, with a particular concern with participatory modes of decision-making and governance. They both strive for the articulation of strategies and plans that are comprehensive and integrated in nature. They both share a longer-term orientation and focus on developmental outcomes. And they are both underpinned by the notion of local ownership of the strategies that are formulated, albeit in relation to different spatial points of reference. The question is whether this emphasis on process has come at the expense of limited attention to certain areas of content, such as migration. Also, where explicit reference is made to migration in these strategic planning frameworks, the manner in which it is treated needs to be scrutinised.

For the purpose of this analysis, the most recent versions of the Integrated Development Plans (IDPs) of South Africa's six metropolitan municipalities are examined. These are the City of Johannesburg, the City of Tshwane, and Ekurhuleni in Gauteng Province, the City of Cape Town in the Western Cape, eThekwini in KwaZulu-Natal, and Nelson Mandela in the Eastern Cape. Annex 2 provides a detailed profile of the coverage of migration in the reviewed IDPs.

City of Johannesburg

In its profile and development overview, the City of Johannesburg's 2004-2005 IDP uses official statistics to provide empirical evidence of patterns of urbanisation and migration.[229] Between 1996 and 2001, the population of Gauteng province rose by 1.4 million, with the province being the destination of more than half of the population flows out of Limpopo, KwaZulu-Natal and Mpumalanga. A large portion of these migrants are reportedly skilled and in possession of a matric certificate or higher qualification. The city's lower than average unemployment rate and the prospect of job opportunities is cited as an attraction to unemployed migrants, placing pressure on the unemployment rate in Johannesburg.[230] The IDP also states that the rate of in-migration to the city is outpacing the delivery of housing and basic household services, resulting in backlogs.[231]

The policy strategies in the City of Johannesburg's IDP are grouped into seven sectors: HIV/AIDS, city safety, economic development, environmental management, water services, housing and disaster management.[232] Migration issues are mentioned in only two of these policy action areas - water services and housing - and are clearly conceived as a challenge for city planners in meeting service delivery targets. In the former instance, a high population growth rate in the municipal area, which the plan ascribes to internal and international in-migration, is producing "exceedingly high short-term growth in water demand."[233] A similar theme emerges in relation to the city's housing strategy, with rapid in-migration to Johannesburg being classified as a potential threat to the city's development framework, vision, and limited available resources to effect change.[234] On a more positive note, the municipality aims to convert single sex hostels, which came to symbolise the migratory labour system under apartheid, into a mixed form of accommodation.[235]

Migration is again referred to in a subsequent chapter, which summarises the business plans compiled by the departments, utilities, agencies and companies.[236] The importance of Johannesburg as the country's premier business node is noted as having contributed to migration patterns that have increased the city's population and intensified the demand for services. More specifically, the migration of people to the inner city and neighbouring localities is seen as challenge to the provision of public bus transportation, while the relationship between urbanisation, population growth and the mounting demand for housing is identified as a threat to conservation areas such as city parks.

Finally, in discussing the envisaged Performance Management System for the city, migrants are listed as a specific vulnerable group that the proposed Human Development Agenda (HDA), a policy framework that will be created so that the City can begin to tackle issues regarding poverty and quality of life, will aim to assist.[237]

City of Tshwane

In providing a profile of the City of Tshwane Metropolitan Municipality (CTMM) area, population movement features quite prominently and a reasonably detailed spatial analysis is provided.[238] Apartheid spatial engineering deferred processes of urbanization, with influx control policies biasing labour mobility and producing dense peri-urban dormitory settlements on the city's border. This served to polarise the majority of the city's inhabitants residing in the poor, remote north-western areas and the more affluent population in the south and east. The plan notes that this spatial inequality is increasing as new economic opportunities develop to the south and east of the city centre rather than to the north.[239] The poor neighbourhoods have the lowest provision of social facilities, the longest travelling times to the city core, the highest population density, and the fastest population growth rate. Other patterns of mobility discussed in the IDP include the sizable number of commuters who reside in Tshwane and work in Johannesburg, contributing to the expansion of residential areas in the southern and south-eastern corridor, as well as the flow of unskilled and semi-skilled labour from North-West and Limpopo Provinces into the northern part of Tshwane.[240]

Several of the major challenges and threats articulated for the CTMM-area touch on migration issues. The first of these is the inefficient regional mobility routing system, with a relative absence of major routes in the west, where more than half the population and the majority of the poor reside. Second, it is recognised that the brain drain amongst the more skilled sectors of the city's economy necessitates the development of a skills training and mentorship programme. Finally, a concern is expressed with regard to the pressure that population growth and urbanization could place on Tshwane's environmental resources.[241]

Although the Tshwane IDP does engage with migration factors and their link to poverty, the prioritized policy actions are not especially sensitive to migration dynamics. The development of the poor, dislocated northern parts of Tshwane is mentioned to varying degrees under transport development, emergency services, housing, services (stormwater management and sanitation), HIV/AIDS and social development. However, explicit reference to migration patterns is only made in relation to disaster management.[242] The IDP rather negatively states that poverty, population growth and rapid urbanization has placed considerable pressure on infrastructure and resulted in an escalation of societal conflict, crime and health hazards, which in turn has heightened vulnerability to disasters.[243]

Migration is mentioned in two other sections of the plan. Firstly, in assessing Tshwane's *First Revised IDP*, a detailed spatial analysis of the present and possible future population movements to, from and within the municipality was conducted, including the implications for service provision and job creation.[244] The second reference is in relation to the IDP Needs Register, which is a system of identifying, categorizing and collecting the development needs of wards and accurately linking them to integrated plans, policies and programmes.[245] Migration concerns are mentioned in the list of needs specified by four Ward Committees. These focused on housing and settlement management, with community requests including the need for "proper control of the influx of refugees", the "moving of illegal immigrants to formal housing" and dealing with "homelessness due to refugees."

Ekurhuleni

The Ekurhuleni IDP only makes cursory reference to migration.[246] Conspicuously absent from the municipal contextual profile, migration is raised in several instances in the section of the plan that describes operational strategies. Here, however, population movement is mostly construed as a threat to development processes. The uncoordinated influx of people and population growth is perceived as a threat to municipal infrastructure. In respect of community services, rapid urbanization is associated with an increasing demand for housing subsidies, uncontrolled settlement formation, and mounting pressure on health and developmental social services. "Illegal immigrants" and rapid urbanization are designated as threats to public safety, with population movement being characterised as a source of crime.

Cape Town

Two documents were reviewed for the City of Cape Town, namely the Draft Integrated Development Plan 2004/2005 and the Integrated Development Plan 2005/2006.[247] In the Draft 2004/2005 IDP, migration issues are not addressed in the municipality's situational analysis, though they are discussed in two of the six prioritized policy strategies. The strategy of shifting growth to the urban core acknowledges that housing and service delivery for the poor over the past decade has created large dormitory settlements of low-cost mass housing on the urban periphery, which has resulted in a lack of employment and recreational opportunities, long travelling times, and continued race and income-based segregation.[248] The advocated strategy promotes mixed use, mixed income, high-density development in well-located and accessible areas that are already serviced by current infrastructure in order to create new opportunities for lower income families. Secondly, the strategy on improving access and mobility emphasizes improvement in the management and operations of public transport in the city in order to facilitate access of the poor to employment and recreational opportunities.[249] In addition, the Draft IDP raises concerns about the insufficient financial resource base of the city to meet the demands imposed by the growing in-migration of largely poor people from rural and other urban areas. In response to the high numbers of new migrants, it recognizes the need to scale up the provision of basic services, skills development and social grants, as well as promote more compact designs that increase residential densities, reduce long-distance commuting, and help overcome spatial disjunctures.[250]

The recently released *Integrated Development Plan 2005/2006* does mark a slight departure, especially given the introduction of a section on population growth and migration into its situational analysis. On the one hand the IDP outlines how significant investment in basic services has only just kept pace with household growth, which is partly attributable to the movement of large numbers of poor people into the city.[251] However, on the other hand, and somewhat progressively, the IDP accepts this tension between population growth and growing service backlogs as an "inevitable result of urbanisation and economic development."[252] Accordingly, city management must prioritise the management of urban growth in order to "integrate new migrants into the city as quickly as possible in terms of accessing services, housing and economic opportunities." As for policy strategies, the 2005/2006 IDP retains the theme of access and mobility, noting that increased demands are to be met by means of a range of programmes directed at significantly improving public transport. Finally, despite some improvement in the migration content and analysis of the IDP, in-migration from rural areas is still understood as a challenge that will impact the city's financial resources, while migrant labour and urbanisation are seen as factors fuelling HIV/AIDS and TB in Cape Town.[253]

eThekwini Municipality

Migration is not a theme that has been strongly incorporated into the eThekwini municipality's integrated development planning processes over the last few years. The *Integrated Development Plan 2003-2007* makes no explicit mention of migration issues, either in its contextual analysis or subsequent policy actions.[254] The *Reviewed Integrated Development Plan 2003-2007* includes an equally partial treatment of migration.[255] Migrants and refugees are identified, in the section on Health and Empowered Citizens, as a special risk group whose interests and needs are to be addressed by the Municipality.[256] However, the failure to systematically analyse the situation of these mobile populations (and other at-risk groups) is reflected in the lack of specification of the policy actions required to effectively address their needs.

Nelson Mandela Metropolitan Municipality

The *Integrated Development Plan* that was produced by the Nelson Mandela Metropolitan Municipality in 2003 does not reflect migration issues in its municipality profile and only occasionally cites them as part of the sector priorities in the development strategy.[257] As part of its Housing and Land Portfolio, the municipality expresses an intention to consider special housing programmes for special groups, including immigrants, street-children and AIDS orphans.[258] However, more negatively and in common with several of the other IDPs, population growth due to in-migration is perceived as a risk to existing municipal infrastructure, while the physical expansion of the metropolitan area is seen as generating barriers to mobility and transportation. In response, an urgent costing of a long-term programme to develop public transport and road infrastructure systems is recommended.[259] Lastly, in relation to the IDP budget, limited financial resources coupled with urbanisation represents challenges that strain infrastructure, service delivery and developmental projects. An emphasis is consequently placed on identifying non-traditional sources of revenue and other resources to ensure the continued sustainability of developmental projects and services.[260]

Namibia

Despite data limitations, research has shown that there are four major patterns of internal migration in Namibia.[261] Rural-rural migration within the communal areas emerges as the most significant, accounting for more than half of lifetime migration and between 26%-34% of first through fourth moves. This form of migration is especially pronounced in the rural north. Rural-urban migration accounts for an estimated 15% of lifetime migration, 24% of first time moves and 7% of fourth moves. This pattern involves moves from rural communal areas to urban communal towns as well as to urban central towns (especially Windhoek). Urban-urban migration constitutes approximately 20% of lifetime migration, and between 20-28% of first through fourth moves. Finally, urban-rural migration makes up about 9% of lifetime migration and between 8-24% of first to fourth moves. There is some evidence of circular migration underlying this trend, with people born in the rural north returning after spending time in urban areas. Cross-border migration accounts for an estimated 6% of lifetime migration in Namibia. In-migration is more significant than outward flows, due primarily to returnees from exile following independence. The dominant cross-border migration flows appear to be urban white and coloured people migrating to South Africa, and rural north communal dwellers migrating to Angola and southern Zambia.[262]

With regard to temporal dynamics, there are signs that migration patterns have undergone significant change since Namibia received independence from South Africa in 1990. In particular, urbanisation in the country is occurring at a fairly rapid pace, producing notable urban growth rates in Windhoek and secondary towns. Clear evidence of the urbanizing character of the population comes from census data, which shows that the percentage of Namibians residing in rural localities declined from about 70% in 1990 to nearly 65% in 1996.[263] The implication of this is a need for decision-makers to develop policy to ensure that social service delivery keeps apace with urbanisation.

Since independence, a number of official policy documents have set out to address the poverty challenge facing the country. The *First National Development Plan* (NDP1), which covered the period 1995/6-1999/00, cited poverty reduction as one of four national development objectives, and contained explicit targets for reducing the incidence of poverty over the period of the plan. This was followed by the release of the *Poverty Reduction Strategy for Namibia* (PRS), which was approved by Cabinet in December 1998 and provides an analysis of the incidence and causes of poverty, and proposes strategies to address it. More specifically, the PRS focuses on fostering more equitable and efficient delivery of public services, accelerating equitable agricultural expansion, and exploring options for non-agricultural economic empowerment (especially in the informal sector and through self-employment).[264] It also articulates social protection policies for the vulnerable in the form of labour intensive public works and the strengthening of grant-based transfer programmes.

After ratifying the PRS, Cabinet approved a process for formulating a *National Poverty Reduction Action Programme* (NPRAP). This was finally approved by Cabinet in October 2001 and represents an elaboration of the PRS. The NPRAP retains the same directions and priority areas as the PRS, but goes on to specify 62 detailed actions and targets deemed necessary to ensure effective implementation. The document identifies programmes, projects and services that focus on poverty reduction over a five-year period, between 2001 and 2005.[265] These activities were integrated into the *Second National Development Plan* (NDP2), which covers the period 2001-2006 and contains an explicit chapter on poverty reduction. The NPRAP also differs from the PRS in that it advocates the mainstreaming of poverty reduction actions into the line functions of relevant ministries and regional councils, the participation of other external stakeholders in the formulation, implementation and assessment of poverty reduction activities, and the incorporation of the gender dimensions of poverty.

The *Poverty Reduction Strategy* (1998) identified recent migrants into marginalized urban areas as one of a number of groups that are disproportionately impoverished in Namibia.[266] In a chapter outlining the developmental challenges facing the country, reference is made to the salience of remittances as an income source.[267] Furthermore, a strong emphasis is placed on the twin dynamics of rapid population growth and processes of urbanisation, raising concerns about 'rural distress' and 'urban dysfunction'. The particular example of Windhoek is cited. The city's population has trebled over the last three decades, largely due to in-migration from the North-Central regions, resulting in apprehension over water scarcity.[268]

The theme of urbanisation is again revisited in a subsequent chapter detailing the long-term vision for a prosperous Namibia. Recognising that urbanisation is likely to continue, the strategy document speculates that within 25 years, the majority of the country's population is likely to have migrated to urban centres. As such, the document suggests that an integrated poverty reduction strategy is needed to ensure that the urban centres are capable of providing sufficient employment opportunities and decent living wages. It also advocates urgent investment in the development of a transport and manufacturing hub, as well as in human capital. Apart from this, migration remains conspicuously absent from the sections of the policy document relating to proposed strategies to meet the country's poverty challenge.

The *National Poverty Reduction Action Plan*, despite being a more fleshed out version of the PRS, fails to mainstream migration into the policy content. As with the PRS, it acknowledges the vulnerability to poverty of recent migrants into marginalized urban areas.[269] It also mentions the role of inequality in living standards between rural and urban as a strong incentive for rural-urban migration. The result is the expansion of informal settlements in most of the country's urban centres.[270] However, research by the Southern African Migration Project has shown that living standards are actually a relatively less common reason for rural-urban migration (7-12% of first through fourth moves) than family reasons, economic issues and education.[271] The PRSAP also equates male migration patterns with increasing numbers and vulnerability of female-headed households.[272] With regard to policy proposals, mobile schools that follow the pastoral nomads in the northern Kunene region are mentioned as one of a number of interventions attempting to promote school enrolment and human capital development.[273]

Both the PRS and PRSAP stress the significance of the *National Population Policy for Sustainable Human Development* (1997) as part of the long-term vision for addressing poverty in Namibia, particularly the measures aimed at facilitating a balanced development of rural and urban areas in order to prevent excessive urbanisation. In common with many of the previously discussed poverty reduction strategies from the region, Namibia's population policy concentrates on stemming rather than managing urbanward migration flows, as is demonstrated by the call for "integrated rural and urban development ...in order to reduce the rate of rural-to-urban migration and forestall parasitic urbanisation."[274] There is no other explicit mention of migration in the remainder of the strategic content of the PRSAP, which addresses income generation, social protection, and public resource management.

The poverty reduction chapter in the *Second National Development Plan*, which draws substantively on both the PRS and PRSAP, is also rather disappointing in terms of the poor representation of migration issues in the proposed sector strategies. As with the other two documents, only passing reference is made to the risk of poverty that confronts recent migrants to urban centres and disparities in rural and urban living standards as a determinant of rural-urban flows.[275]

Swaziland

Swaziland has a rich migration history, with labour migration to South Africa dating back to the late nineteenth century.[276] Migration streams have traditionally been male, due to the demand of South African mines and patriarchal attitudes towards the roles of women. By the 1990s, the principal domestic employment opportunities for Swazis were in commercial agriculture, manufacturing and services, while external migrants were principally employed by the South African mines (despite increasing retrenchments) and to a lesser extent agribusiness and tourism in Mpumalanga province, and manufacturing and domestic service in Gauteng and Mpumalanga provinces. In the post-1990 period, with the transition to democracy in South Africa, patterns of cross-border migration have undergone notable change. The number of people traveling to South Africa each year has more than quadrupled, as the end of apartheid made South Africa a more attractive place to visit for tourism or business purposes. Other changes included an upward trend in work-seeking migrants in South Africa (both documented and undocumented) due to declining economic conditions in Swaziland, a 'brain drain' of skilled Swazis to South Africa's health and education sectors, and a substantial increase in predominantly female cross-border trading.[277]

Swaziland's *Poverty Reduction Strategy and Action Plan* (PRSAP) is the most recent national poverty reduction strategy to emerge in Southern Africa, with the two-volume draft document being placed on the government's web portal in December 2005.[278] Given the recency of the strategy, policymakers and other stakeholders involved in the formulation process might have drawn lessons from the collective experience of other countries in the sub-region and addressed some of the well-documented shortcomings that characterize their poverty reduction strategies. While the analysis of the content of the PRSAP documents does indicate that migration has been incorporated into the country's poverty profile, policy framework, macroeconomic framework, and action programme, the nature of its inclusion is limited.

Given the intense and long-established migration trends between Swaziland and South Africa, it is unsurprising that the PRSAP mentions remittances and diminished cross-border employment opportunities in the section detailing the nature of poverty in the country. More specifically, the documents discuss how only two percent of the income of the country's rural poor is derived from remittances, with wage income remaining the predominant source. However, concern is raised over the extent to which employment opportunities have declined during the 1990s, in part attributable to mineworker retrenchments in South Africa, and the impact that this may have on the livelihoods and survival of poor households.[279] This is brought into focus in a subsequent section which describes how poor families are dependent on wage and remitted income, but are simultaneously the most vulnerable to retrenchment. Another section discusses how poor families struggle to grow enough food and depend on remittances to buy food packages and ensure their food security. While drawing attention to these vulnerabilities is important, what is missing is a reflection on contemporary migration streams, and how these alleviate or exacerbate the situation. For instance, there is no consideration of the increasing feminization of migration and the role that female cross-border traders serve in helping impoverished families to cope during difficult economic conditions.

As with a number of poverty reduction strategies in the sub-region, Swaziland's PRSAP mentions the need to control, curb and even reverse migration flows, especially from rural to urban areas. The report links the process of urbanisation over the last few decades with urban unemployment, the rise in unplanned settlements without public infrastructure and services, crime and the number of street children.[280] Rural-urban migration is considered one of the factors driving overpopulation, overgrazing, and diminishing farm sizes, which in turn is exacerbating environmental problems such as soil erosion, deforestation and forest degradation and water and air pollution.[281] In response, investment in rural infrastructure (roads, bridges, electricity, water, industrial parks, telecommunications) is advocated as a national priority and a means to improving investment opportunities in rural areas, creating jobs and ultimately reducing rural-urban migration.[282] Similarly, to reduce the need to migrate to cities, community tourism is promoted as a way of generating employment opportunities, while the construction of extra factory shells in rural areas is seen as a way of encouraging small and medium enterprise development.[283] Improving conditions in rural localities is considered an appropriate approach to countering the rapid growth of informal urban settlements.[284]

Migration does feature quite prominently in the section on HIV/AIDS. Swaziland has the highest estimated adult prevalence rate in the world, and has not shown signs of stabilization, a phenomenon that characterizes many other countries in sub-Saharan Africa.[285] Risk assessments in the country illustrate the salient role that migration plays in the transmission of HIV/AIDS.[286] Reflecting such findings, the PRSAP cites internal migration as an explanatory variable in understanding equally high rural and urban prevalence rates. The migration of family breadwinners to towns or to neighbouring South Africa in search of employment is seen to increase the likelihood of risky sexual behaviour and HIV infection. Urbanisation and labour migration are also seen as adversely affecting traditional mechanisms for coping with shocks such as HIV/AIDS. For instance, migration erodes the ability of extended families to absorb orphans and very young children from AIDS-affected households.[287]

The final domain in which migration issues are incorporated pertains to immigration into Swaziland. As recent attitudinal research has shown, Swazis tend to assign blame for high unemployment rates on foreigners, especially during times of economic hardship or uncertainty, even though the evidence supporting this claim is illusory.[288] In addition, there is fairly strong support for restrictionism in Swazi immigration policy, with two-thirds expressing a desire for the government to strictly limit the number of foreigners entering the country, and nearly 80 percent supporting the deportation of irregular immigrants.[289] Such attitudes appear to have informed the formulation of the PRSAP. The strategy document raises concern over the level of irregular migrants to the country, which is perceived to place increasing pressure on social services, natural resources and the economy.[290] The Government subsequently outlines its intention to intensify efforts to curb 'illegal immigration', through measures such as the strengthening of border immigration controls. The expectation is that such interventions will help to improve the quality of life of the poor by reducing the demand for, and improving their chances of accessing, land, services, employment, and so forth.[291] Acknowledging the informal economy as an important livelihood source for many poor and unemployed Swazis (including returnee migrant workers), the document further states that the government aims to provide support by regulating or even eliminating sub-standard goods coming from foreign countries through illegal cross-border movements.[292]

Ironically, while popular sentiment favours strict controls on the movement of goods and people into Swaziland, there is conversely a demand for the relaxing of South African immigration policy.[293] This contradiction is again mirrored in the PRSAP. Despite advocating a hardening of controls on the Swaziland side, the document also promotes the adoption of measures that would facilitate the mobility of labour between Swaziland and other countries in the region in order to stimulate trade.[294] These findings suggest the need to reappraise the country's immigration policy, as the move towards increasing restriction does seem incompatible with greater regional integration. In addition, effort will have to be exerted to communicate that there is no direct relationship between the presence of immigrants and the country's economic woes.

Chapter

5 RECOMMEN-DATIONS FOR MAINSTREAMING MIGRATION

This report has examined poverty reduction strategies in Southern Africa with a view to gaining an appreciation of the level of understanding of the potentially positive role that migration can play in reducing poverty.[295] This chapter summarizes some of the themes that emerged from the preceding analysis. It will also discuss their implications for ongoing processes of pro-poor policy formulation and implementation at the regional, national and sub-national levels.

Migration in Poverty Reduction Strategies in Southern Africa

From an international perspective, population stability was historically seen as the norm and migration within, between and from developing countries was viewed by governments as an indicator of severe social collapse and an indictment of the state's ability to provide people with an adequate quality of life in their country of origin.[296] This negative view of migration became more deeply entrenched in the latter half of the twentieth century, as rapid urbanisation in newly independent countries provoked fear that the economy and local government would be "overwhelmed by the numbers of migrants and the spread of vast squatter settlements and shanty towns."[297] However, parallel to this, evidence mounted of the importance of migration as a livelihood strategy, and the role of remittance flows as a means of redistributing income and reducing vulnerability.[298]

The emergence of what has been termed the 'new poverty agenda' during the 1990s transformed the approach to the needs of developing countries, with poverty reduction now firmly placed as the overarching objective. This new focus on poverty reduction draws together the Millennium Development Goals, an international consensus on how to reduce poverty, Poverty Reduction Strategy Papers and a new set of instruments for delivering aid.[299]

These developments raise important policy questions:

- Is there recognition in the SADC of the positive aspects of migration, rather than a continual focus on the problems and challenges that it poses?

- Are we beginning to see a reversal of policy in Southern Africa, with governments dispensing with attempts to restrict migration?

- Are policies becoming more openly supportive of population mobility and do they incorporate measures to protect migrants against exploitation and discrimination?

This review of SADC poverty strategies provides rather disappointing answers to these questions, suggesting that migration is still not receiving the attention it deserves.

At the regional level, there are encouraging signs that migration is being increasingly treated as a salient issue in relation to poverty reduction and development.[300] The establishment of the Migration Dialogue for Southern Africa (MIDSA) is particularly significant in this respect. The institution was established in late 2000 by the International Organisation for Migration (IOM) and the Southern African Migration Project.[301] The primary objectives of MIDSA are to encourage regional consultation and cooperation on migration issues, and develop regional capacity to address migration issues and strengthen the ability of governments to address migration in a comprehensive and integrated manner.[302] Activities undertaken through this process have a potentially transformative agenda include ongoing efforts to promote the positive dimensions of migration amongst SADC and COMESA member states, and a forum in 2004 on migration and development which facilitated discussion amongst senior officials and policymakers on the nexus between migration and poverty reduction.[303]

Yet, in spite of these welcome steps, there remains considerable room for progress in ensuring that any new awareness and more nuanced understanding of migration resulting from regional consultative processes are actively and sufficiently integrated into regional and national development policy. As previously discussed, the Regional Indicative Strategic Development Plan unfortunately does not make explicit reference to migration as a key priority area. Migration does, however, feature as an implicit cross-cutting issue in all priority intervention areas and numerous policy issues likely to exert an influence on migration are identified.

At the national level, the treatment of migration issues in poverty reduction strategies is relatively inconsistent and decidedly partial. Of the six Southern African countries with either interim of full Poverty Reduction Strategy Papers, migration is practically ignored in the national poverty profiles of two countries (Tanzania, Zambia) and is both circumscribed and negatively perceived in a further three cases (Mozambique, Malawi, Lesotho). For example, migration is seen as promoting the spread of crime and diseases such as HIV/AIDS (Malawi), placing undue pressure on urban areas (Mozambique, Lesotho) limiting employment opportunities (Malawi, Mozambique), and contributing to the breakdown of family structures (Malawi, Lesotho). Only Lesotho seems to mention migration as a positive factor in its poverty profile, indicating the importance of remittances in preventing poverty and expressing concern over the declining availability of jobs in South Africa's mines. Still, even here there is ambivalence, with declining urban-based conditions, services and quality of life being attributed to internal migration. The two conflict-affected countries in the region that have embarked on the PRSP process (Angola, DRC) remain somewhat exceptional in that the demands for the reintegration and resettlement of internally displaced and refugee populations tend to predominate the poverty reduction strategies.

Reflecting this relatively scant and negative handling of migration in the poverty profiles, the Southern African PRSPs also offer uneven policy and programmatic responses that either directly address migration or have an indirect influence on mobile populations. This tends to confirm that if issues such as migration "are not brought up at the diagnostic stage, it is very unlikely that they will appear in the 'action' or 'monitoring' stages."[304] Where migration is mentioned there is often very little appreciation of the different migration flows in the given country context. Certain types of migration stream are also conspicuously missing. With the exception of the region's poor, conflict-affected countries, there is hardly any discussion of refugee populations, even for those countries that are known to have been host to large refugee populations in the last decade (e.g. Tanzania, Zambia). This tends to corroborate similar evidence of neglect found in other reviews of PRSPs.[305]

Although they do not qualify for formal, World Bank/IMF endorsed PRSPs, most of the middle income countries in Southern Africa (Botswana, Namibia, South Africa, Swaziland, Seychelles and Mauritius) have either completed or are busy formulating national poverty reduction strategies. Since most of these are not readily available, this review has focused exclusively on South Africa as a case study. The results should therefore be considered indicative and subject to follow-up verification and research. South Africa does however provide a useful policy context warranting in-depth examination for several reasons. It is a significant migrant-receiving country in the sub-region, but is also typified by noteworthy internal and international migration dynamics. Since democracy in 1994, there has been a proliferation and evolution of different policy frameworks that aim to address post-apartheid poverty and development challenges. These developmental policies operate at different spatial levels, ranging from the national to the municipal, and provide an opportunity to gain insight into the extent to which there is internal consistency in the coverage and treatment of migration between policies crafted by different tiers of government.

With regard to national policy, South Africa's 1994 Reconstruction and Development Programme (RDP) did advocate a balanced approach that incorporated interventions in both urban and rural localities. It acknowledged that economic migration would remain an enduring feature of the country and a salient livelihood strategy, and made a series of recommendations that would ensure that the needs of these mobile populations would be served. An inconsistent and slightly less favourable message was communicated with respect to cross-border migration into the country, with the government specifying the need for regional development as a means of effectively preventing these population flows. The document further suffered from a lack of precision in many instances, with migration generally portrayed in an undifferentiated manner. Migration coverage in the RDP somehow diminished in the progression from the original Base Document to the subsequent White Paper.[306] The emergence of the Growth, Employment and Redistribution programme did little to reverse this trend.[307] The five-year, market-led strategy became the central component of the government's anti-poverty strategy, with privatization, liberalization and deficit reduction being advanced as the means to stimulate the economy, create jobs and ultimately assist in reducing poverty and inequality. In the process, migration effectively disappeared from the national development policy agenda. The Integrated Sustainable Rural Development and the Urban Renewal Programmes, introduced in 2000, do emphasise the need to consider complex, rural-urban linkages in planning for development, though this imperative has been insufficiently reflected in the programmatic visions and measures.

At the sub-national level, the dominant policy instruments for development planning and poverty reduction are the Provincial Growth and Development Strategies and the municipality-level Integrated Development Plans. Both were introduced in 1996 and have been through consecutive and ongoing rounds of refinement. At the provincial level, the review indicates that certain similarities exist between the different growth and development plans in their engagement with migration. Again the evidence is not very reassuring. The documents examined are generally weak in their inclusion of migration and, where mentioned, is informed by negative or dualistic attitudes.

With regard to Integrated Development Plans of the metropolitan municipalities, there is substantial variation in both the scope and nature of migration related content. Some of these documents do provide relatively good coverage (Johannesburg, Tshwane, Cape Town). Yet, even in these cases, there are important disparities between the contextual profiles and prioritized development strategies. In the latter, migration tends to be generally more circumscribed and negatively framed, with the challenges of meeting the infrastructure, shelter and community service needs of fast growing populations predominating. Evidence from the IDPs of other metropolitan municipalities (Nelson Mandela, eThekwini and Ekurhuleni) is less encouraging, with only cursory mention of migration. This is not necessarily a reflection of actual demographic processes and trends. For instance, Ekurhuleni was the country's fastest growing population of any South African city between 1996 an 2001, and might be expected to address migration issues in a more thorough and deliberate manner.[308]

Some IDPs have displayed distinct signs of improvement between successive versions (e.g Cape Town), while others remain resolutely indifferent to migration (e.g. eThekwini). There are also significant gaps that include the tendency (a) to overlook empirical evidence on demographic change (with the exception of Johannesburg) in developing contextual profiles and strategies; (b) to generalise rather than provide a nuanced characterization of migration flows; and (c) to omit or harshly view certain types of migrant (especially irregular migrants and refugees).

Therefore, as the South African case reveals, in considering migration and poverty reduction policies the focus should not exclusively be on the regional and national level. The textured, inconsistent and highly variable nature with which migration is reflected in national and sub-national policy documents means that there is a need for a coordinated approach to mainstreaming migration which reaches from the regional down to the local level.

Towards a Transformative Agenda

Despite growing international and regional awareness of the critical relationship between development and migration, there has not yet emerged a coherent and coordinated policy approach to poverty reduction in the Southern African sub-region that reflects this thinking. Instead, and as discussed at length in preceding chapters, poverty reduction strategies and developmental policies at the regional, national and sub-national level tend to exhibit an assumption that "the relationship between migration and poverty is negative: migration is the result of deprivation or it leads to the impoverishment of certain areas."[309]

Indirect and Unintended Policy Consequences

This view of the impoverishing and destabilising effect of migration both for migrants and source households and localities lends itself to the advocacy of restrictive policy mechanisms that dissuade or control population movement.[310] This is implicit in the current focus of rural development and poverty reduction policies on agricultural growth and pro-poor tourism as employment generating schemes that would inhibit migratory tendencies. This focus fails to address recent findings on the multi-locational nature of livelihoods, with migration representing a regular, often accumulative livelihood strategy for numerous poor people in the region rather than merely a product of rural distress.[311]

While acknowledging the returns brought by migration, especially in consideration of remittances and the possible multiplier effects of these contributions, the decision to move can expose migrants to a range of vulnerabilities. These include the financial cost of migrating (such as transportation and rents), poor access to basic services, insecurity of tenure, and the risk of exploitation, harassment and abuse. Numerous government programmes, even those without explicit reference to migration, are likely to have indirect or unintended consequences for migrants. The danger is that with the relative neglect and neutral or hostile treatment of migration in poverty reduction strategies, migrants become incidental beneficiaries or victims of proposed policy and pro-grammatic interventions.[312] This suggests the need for migration-friend-ly development policies that are directed towards supporting migration as a poverty-reducing measure for both source and destination areas or countries, by facilitating the contributory role of remittances while concomitantly protecting migrants from abuse and exploitation.

Knowledge Gaps

Part of the problem is the insufficient migration data with which to inform a culture of evidence-based policy making. There have admit-tedly been notable recent advances in the availability of basic informa-tion on the causes, consequences and outcomes of migration decisions over the last decade.[313] Lingering issues nonetheless remain, including the uneven coverage, scope and quality of migration research within Southern Africa, as well as the periodicity of migration surveys. There is, therefore, a need to scale up policy-oriented research on the pov-erty-migration linkage in the region, building upon the work on this subject that has been undertaken by the Southern African Migration Project and others. If this is not prioritised then the lack of migration data is likely to continue to constrain our understanding, monitoring and assessment of internal, intra-, and extra-regional migration levels and trends and adversely affect our ability to make informed policy decisions.[314] It is also likely to influence the extent to which the rights of migrants are protected in ongoing efforts to scale up poverty reduc-tion programmes to make progress towards meeting the Millennium Development Goals and long-term national goals.

Challenging Perspectives

Another related issue is the fact that the knowledge base on migration that does exist is being weakly incorporated into poverty policy in the region. The negative assumptions of many poverty reduction strategies are therefore not supported by empirical evidence. In fact, recent evidence does tend to point to the potential role of migration in reducing poverty and dispels a number of myths surrounding population movement. It is important that in formulating poverty reduction strategies, the potentially positive role that migration can fulfil is appropriately accommodated. Not only does this translate into the need for the collection of more reliable and timely data, but it also requires ongoing support to initiatives such as the Migration Dialogue for Southern Africa as a means of increasing awareness amongst policymakers. The latter has the potential to progressively ensure that migration features in the regional and national development agendas and provides the impetus for moving towards the adoption of a coherent approach that treats migration in a suitably balanced and differentiated manner.

This regional dialogue should, however, be accompanied by similar consultative efforts at the national and sub-national levels. In particular, the role of non-governmental stakeholders in ensuring that the needs of migrant populations are effectively incorporated into pro-poor policy needs to be emphasized. Yet, it is equally crucial that efforts be exerted to make certain that, where possible, the voices of a range of different types of migrants are directly represented in future participatory processes that are undertaken to inform the design of national poverty reduction strategies.

In moving forward and ensuring that migration issues are more systematically integrated by national development policy formulation teams, a clear analytical framework for understanding migration in the national and regional context is required. This should be produced together with a set of region-specific guidelines for producing poverty reduction strategies that are migration-sensitive in all the core dimensions (diagnostics, strategy, monitoring and evaluation).

Scope for Change

The success of efforts to promote the articulation of poverty reduction strategies that capture the benefits of migration for poverty reduction is ultimately influenced by the extent to which there are inherent flexibilities built into policy planning and implementation processes. Fortunately, in their design, the region's poverty reduction strategies appear to be underscored by an iterative approach. The Regional Indicative Strategic Development Plan has been conceived as a 'living document' that is both flexible and adaptable, while the Poverty Reduction Strategy Paper (PRSP) approach is configured such that countries produce a new document every three years. In the South African context, the preparation of a Provincial Growth and Development Strategy is similarly viewed as an iterative process that "must be updated on a regular basis as new information and insights become available and policies impacting on development are refined and clarified."[315] The country's integrated development planning process is still in its infancy and evolutionary in nature, improving progressively alongside the expansion of local government capacity.[316] There is thus cause for optimism about the prospects for mainstreaming migration, since the flexibility of the strategy documents presents an opportunity for incorporating migration issues more systematically in ongoing rounds of updating, revision and implementation.

Notes

1   Jonathan Crush, Vincent Williams and Sally Peberdy, "Migration in Southern Africa", Paper prepared for the Policy Analysis and Research Programme of the Global Commission on International Migration, September 2005; John Oucho, "Cross-Border Migration and Regional Initiatives in Managing Migration in Southern Africa" In Pieter Kok, Derik Gelderblom, John Oucho and Johan Van Zyl (eds.) *Migration in South and Southern Africa: Dynamics and Determinants*, (Cape Town: HSRC Press, 2005), pp.47-70.

2   Crush, Williams and Peberdy, "Migration in Southern Africa", p.1; Richard Black, *Migration and Pro-Poor Policies in Africa*, Sussex Centre for Migration Research, DFID, London, 2004, p.59

3   Michael Lipton and Simon Maxwell, *The New Poverty Agenda: An Overview*, Institute of Development Studies, IDS Discussion Paper No. 306, University of Sussex, Brighton, 1992; Simon Maxwell, "Heaven or Hubris: Reflections on the 'New Poverty Agenda'" *Development Policy Review* 21(1) (2003): 5-25.

4   Uma Kothari, "Staying Put and Staying Poor?" *Journal of International Development* 15(5) (2003): 645-657.

5   The RISDP pagination cited in this and subsequent section refers to the version of the document found at the following web address: http://www.sarpn.org.za/documents/d0000294/RISDP_26March2003.pdf (accessed 12.09.2006).

6   Southern African Development Community (SADC) (2004) *Regional Indicative Strategic Development Plan (RISDP)* (Gaborone: SADC Secretariat, 2004), p.119.

7   Ibid, p.105.

8   Ibid, p.119.

9   Ibid, p.130.

10 Ibid, p.7.

11 Ibid, p.119.

12 Prega Ramsamy, The Regional Indicative Strategic Development Plan (RISDP) as a Strategic Framework for Deeper Economic Integration and Social Development in the SADC Region. Available online at: http://www.sadcreview.com/special_features/feature_risdp.htm, 2004.

13 SADC, *Regional Indicative Strategic Development Plan*, pp.76, 89, 99.

14 Ibid, p. 65.

15 Ibid, pp. 27-8.

16 Ibid, p. 99.

17 Colin Fenwick and Evance Kalula, *Law and Labour Market Regulation in East Asia and Southern Africa: Comparative Perspectives*, Centre for Employment and Labour Relations Law Working Paper No.30, University of Melbourne, 2004; John

Oucho and Jonathan Crush, "Contra Free Movement: South Africa and the SADC Migration Protocols" *Africa Today* 48(3) (2001): 139-158.

18   SADC, *Regional Indicative Strategic Development Plan*, p.78.

19   UNAIDS, *2004 Report on the Global AIDS Epidemic: 4th Global Report* (Geneva: UNAIDS, 2004).

20   Tony Barnett and Alan Whiteside, *AIDS in the Twenty-First Century: Disease and Globalisation* (Basingstoke, Hampshire: Palgrave MacMillan, 2002); Jonathan Crush, Brian Williams, Eleanor Gouws and Mark Lurie, "Migration and HIV/AIDS in South Africa" *Development Southern Africa* 22(3) (2005): 293-318.

21   Khangelani Zuma, Eleanor Gouws, Brian Williams and Mark Lurie, "Risk Factors for HIV Infection Among Women in Carltonville, South Africa: Migration, Demography and Sexually Transmitted Diseases" *International Journal of STD and AIDS*, 14(12) (2003): 814-817.

22   Tukufu Zuberi, Amson Sibanda, Ayaga A. Bawah and Amadou Noumbissi, "Population and African Society" *Annual Review of Sociology* 29 (2003): 465-86.

23   Mark Lurie, Brian Williams, Khangelani Zuma, David Mkaya-Mwamburi, Geoff P. Garnett, Micheal D. Sweat, Joel Gittelsohn and Salim S. Abdool Karim, "Who Infects Whom? HIV-1 Concordance and Discordance Among Migrant and Non-Migrant Couples in South Africa" *AIDS* 17(15) (2003): 2245-2252.

24   Mark Lurie, "Migration and AIDS in Southern Africa: A Review" *South African Journal of Science* 96(6) (2000): 343-347; Zuma et al, "Risk Factors for HIV Infection."

25   Paul Spiegel, "HIV Surveillance in Situations of Forced Migration" Paper presented at Workshop on Fertility and Reproductive Health in Humanitarian Crises, Roundtable on the Demography of Forced Migration/Committee on Population, The National Academies of Science, Washington, 23–24 October 2002; UNAIDS, *2004 Report on the Global AIDS Epidemic*.

26   International Organisation for Migration (IOM), *Mobile Populations and HIV/AIDS in the Southern African Region: Recommendations for Action* (Geneva: IOM, 2003a).

27   IOM/UNAIDS/UNDP, *HIV/AIDS Prevention and Care Programmes for Mobile Populations in Africa: An Inventory* (Geneva, 2002).

28   Policy Project, *National and Sector HIV/AIDS Policies in the Member States of the Southern Africa Development Community* (Gaborone: SADC, 2002). The eight countries are Botswana, Lesotho, Mozambique, Namibia, South Africa, Swaziland, Zambia and Zimbabwe.

29   IOM, *Mobile Populations and HIV/AIDS in the Southern African Region*.

30   Ibid.

31   Victoria Hosegood and Kathleen Ford, "The Impact of HIV/AIDS on Children's Living Arrangements and Migration in Rural South Africa" Paper presented at the Conference on African Migration in Comparative Perspective, Johannesburg, South Africa, 4-7 June 2003.

32   Lorraine Young and Nicola Ansell, "Young AIDS Migrants in Southern Africa: Policy Implications for Empowering Children" *AIDS Care* 15(3) (2003): 337-45.

33   Ruth Leger Sivard, *Women: A World Survey* (Washington, D.C: World Priorities, 1995).

34   Deborah Budlender, *Why Should We Care About Unpaid Care Work?* (Harare: UNIFEM, 2004).

35   Elizabeth Francis, "Gender, Migration and Multiple Livelihoods: Cases from Eastern and Southern Africa" *Journal of Development Studies* 38(5) (2002): 167-190.

36   Belinda Dodson, "Women On The Move: Gender and Cross-Border Migration to South Africa from Lesotho, Mozambique and Zimbabwe" In David McDonald (ed.) *On Borders: Perspectives on International Migration in Southern Africa* (New York: St Martin's Press, 2000).

37   Hania Zlotnik, "Migrants' Rights, Forced Migration and Migration Policy in Africa" Paper presented at Conference on African Migration in Comparative Perspective, Johannesburg, South Africa, 4-7 June, 2003, p.6.

38   Peter Gibbon, "The African Growth Opportunities Act and the Global Commodity Chain for Clothing" *World Development* 31(11) (2003): 1809-27; Sanjaya Lall, "FDI, AGOA and Manufactured Exports by a Landlocked, Least Developed African Economy: Lesotho" *Journal of Development Studies* 41(6) (2005): 998–1022.

39   Theresa Ulicki and Jonathan Crush, "Gender, Farmwork and Women's Migration from Lesotho to the New South Africa" In Jonathan Crush and David McDonald (eds.) *Transnationalism and New African Immigration to South Africa*, (Toronto: SAMP and CAAS, 2002).

40   International Organisation for Migration (IOM), *World Migration 2003: Managing Migration — Challenges and Responses for People on the Move* (Geneva: IOM, 2003).

41   Ibid, p.7.

42   Catherine Campbell, *Letting Them Die: Why HIV/AIDS Prevention Programmes Fail* (Cape Town: Double Storey Books, 2003).

43   Susan Forbes Martin, "Women and Migration", Paper prepared for the United Nations Division for the Advancement of Women's (DAW) Consultative Meeting on Migration and Mobility and How this Movement Affects Women, Malmö, Sweden, 2-4 December 2003.

44   Belinda Dodson, *Gender Concerns in South African Migration Policy*, SAMP Migration Policy Brief No. 4, Cape Town, 2001.

45   Arjan de Haan, *Migrants, Livelihoods and Rights: The Relevance of Migration in Development Policies,* Department for International Development, Social Development Department Working Paper No.4, London, 2000, pp.5-6.

46   Sally Peberdy, "Mobile Entrepreneurship: Informal Sector Cross-Border Trade and Street Trade in South Africa" *Development Southern Africa* 17(2) (2000): 201-19.

47   Martin Whiteside, *Neighbours in Development: Livelihood Interactions between Northern*

Mozambique and Southern Malawi (London: DFID, 2002); Chris Ackello-Ogutu and Protase Echessh, *Unrecorded Cross-Border Trade Between Tanzania and Her Neighbours*, USAID Africa Bureau, Office of Sustainable Development Technical Paper No.90, Nairobi, 1998; Isaac J. Minde and Teddie O. Nakhumwa, *Unrecorded Cross-Border Trade Between Malawi and Neighbouring Countries*, USAID Africa Bureau, Office of Sustainable Development Technical Paper No.90, Nairobi, 1998; Jose Luis Macamo, *Unrecorded Cross-Border Trade Between Mozambique and Her Neighbours*, USAID Africa Bureau, Office of Sustainable Development Technical Paper No.88, Nairobi,1999.

48   Sally Peberdy, "Hurdles to Trade? South Africa's Immigration Policy and Informal Sector Cross-Border Traders in the SADC" Paper presented at the SAMP/SARPN/LHR seminar on Regional Integration, Migration and Poverty, 25 April 2002, Pretoria.

49   Peberdy, "Mobile Entrepreneurship."

50   Martin Whiteside, *When the Whole is More than the Sum of the Parts: The Effect of Cross-Border Interactions on Livelihood Security in Southern Malawi and Northern Mozambique* (London: Oxfam, 1998); Macamo, *Unrecorded Cross-Border Trade Between Mozambique and Her Neighbours.*

51   Unity Chari, "Informal Cross-border Trade and Gender" Presentation at the Community Organisations Regional Network (CORN) Workshop on Sustainable Development through Trade, Bronte Hotel, Harare, 11-12 February, 2004.

52   Crush, Williams and Peberdy, "Migration in Southern Africa", p.16.

53   SADC, *Regional Indicative Strategic Development Plan*, p.84.

54   Ibid, p.32.

55   Ibid, p.33.

56   Ibid, p.84.

57   Catherine Cross, "Why Does South Africa Need a Spatial Policy? Population, Migration, Infrastructure and Development" *Journal of Contemporary African Studies* 19(1) (2001): 111-27.

58   Ibid, p.114.

59   Kingdom of Lesotho, *Progress Report on the Millennium Development Goals: The War Against HIV/AIDS* (Maseru, 2003).

60   Ian Pearson, *The National Sanitation Programme in Lesotho: How Political Leadership Achieved Long-Term Results*, Water and Sanitation Program – Africa Region (WSP-AF), Blue Gold Field Note 5, Nairobi, 2002.

61   International Development Committee (IDC), *Migration and Development: How to Make Migration Work for Poverty Reduction. Sixth Report of Session 2003–04, Volume I* (London: House of Commons, 2004), p.62.

62   Cross, "Why does South Africa Need a Spatial Policy?" p.111.

63   Cecilia Tacoli, *Changing Rural-Urban Interactions in Sub-Saharan Africa and their Impact on Livelihoods: A Summary*, International Institute for Environment and Development, Rural-Urban Interactions and Livelihood Strategies Working Paper No.7, London, 2002, p.v.

64   Steve Wiggins, *Regional Issues in Food Security in Southern Africa*, Overseas Development Institute, Forum for Food Security in Southern Africa (FFASA) Theme Paper, London, 2003, p.3.

65   Gertrud Schrieder and Beatrice Knerr, "Labour Migration as a Social Security Mechanism for Smallholder Households in Sub-Saharan Africa: The Case of Cameroon" *Oxford Development Studies* 28(2) (2000): 223-36.

66   Wade Pendleton, Jonathan Crush, Eugene Campbell, Thuso Green, Hamilton Simelane, Dan Tevera and Fion de Vletter, *Migration, Remittances and Development in Southern Africa* SAMP Migration Policy Series, No. 44, 2006.

67   Wiggins, *Regional Issues in Food Security in Southern Africa*, p.25.

68   Pendleton, et al, *Migration, Remittances and Development in Southern Africa*.

69   Bruce Frayne, "Migration and Urban Survival Strategies in Windhoek, Namibia" *Geoforum*, 35 (2004): 489-505.

70   Ibid, p.13.

71   SADC FANR, *Regional Emergency Food Security Assessment Report* (Harare: SADC, 2003).

72   IOM, *Mobile Populations and HIV/AIDS*.

73   Crush, Peberdy and Williams, "Migration in Southern Africa."

74   Ashnie Padarath, Charlotte Chamberlain, David McCoy, Antoinette Ntuli, Mike Rowson and Rene Loewenson, *Health Personnel in Southern Africa: Confronting Maldistribution and Brain Drain*, Health Systems Trust, Equinet Discussion Paper Series 3, Durban, 2003.

75   UNAIDS, *2004 Report on the Global AIDS Epidemic*.

76   Ibid. and Olive Shisana, Elsje Hall, KR Maluleke, Dawid J Stoker, Craig Schwabe, Mark Colvin et al, *The Impact of HIV/AIDS on the Health Sector. National Survey of Health Personnel, Ambulatory and Hospitalised Patients and Health Facilities* (Cape Town: Human Science Research Council, 2003).

77   Katharina Kober and Wim Van Damme, "Scaling up Access to Antiretroviral Treatment in Southern Africa: Who Will Do the Job?" *The Lancet* 364(9428) (2004): 103-7.

78   Shisana et al., *The Impact of HIV/AIDS on the Health Sector*; Abel Chikanda, *Medical Leave: The Exodus of Health Professionals from Zimbabwe*, SAMP Migration Policy Series, No. 34, 2005.

79   A. Thomson, "Medical Exodus Saps South Africa's War on AIDS" *Reuters AlertNet*, 3 February 2003, cited in UNAIDS, *2004 Report on the Global AIDS Epidemic*, p.168; International Organisation for Migration, *World Migration 2003*.

80   Padarath et al, *Health Personnel in Southern Africa*.

81   H Lauring, Action Needed on Brain Drain. *Globaleyes*. Available at http://manila. djh.dk/global/stories/storyReader$98; UNAIDS, *2004 Report on the Global AIDS Epidemic*.

82 Ronald Labonte, Corinne Packer, Nathan Klassen, Arminee Kazanjian, Lars Apland, Justina Adalikwu, Jonathan Crush, Tom McIntosh, Ted Schrecker, Joelle Walker, and David Zakus, *The 'Brain Drain' of Health Professionals from Sub-Saharan Africa to Canada: Findings and Options*, SAMP Migration and Development Series No. 2, 2007.

83 Magda Awases, Akpa R. Gbary, Jennifer Nyoni and Rufaro Chatora, *Migration of Health Professionals in Six Countries: A Synthesis Report* (Kinshasa: WHO Regional Office for Africa, 2004).

84 Ibid, p.x.

85 Ibid, pp.62-3.

86 Amanda Sives, W. John Morgan and Simon Appleton, "Teachers as Community Leaders: The Potential Impact of Teacher Migration on Education for All and Millennium Development Goals" Paper presented at the International Conference on Adult Education and Poverty Reduction: A Global Priority, University of Botswana, 14-16 June, 2004, p.2.

87 Paul Benell, *Teacher Motivation and Incentives in Sub-Saharan Africa and Asia* (Brighton, Knowledge and Skills for Development, 2004).

88 Ibid.

89 Improving Educational Quality Project (IEQ), *What Happened to the Teachers? A Teacher Mobility Study in Mangochi and Balaka Districts, Malawi* (IEQ Malawi, 2000).

90 Bennell, *Teacher Motivation and Incentives in Sub-Saharan Africa and Asia*.

91 Kimberly Ochs, *'Teaching at Risk': Teacher Mobility and Loss in Commonwealth Member States* (London: Commonwealth Secretariat, 2003).

92 Bennell, *Teacher Motivation and Incentives in Sub-Saharan Africa and Asia*.

93 Ibid; Sives et al, *Teachers as Community Leaders*; and Ochs, *'Teaching at Risk'*.

94 Hosegood and Ford, "The Impact of HIV/AIDS on Children's Living Arrangements and Migration".

95 Mark Collinson, Steve Tollman, Kathkleen Kahn, and Sam Clark, "Highly Prevalent Circular Migration: Households, Mobility and Economic Status in Rural South Africa" Paper presented at the Conference on African Migration in Comparative Perspective, Johannesburg, South Africa, 4-7 June 2003; Robert E.B. Lucas, "Migration" In Margaret Grosh and Paul Glewwe (eds.) *Designing Household Survey Questionnaires for Developing Countries: Lessons from 15 years of the Living Standards Measurement Study, Volume 2* (Washington, D.C: World Bank, 2000), pp.49-81.

96 Arjan de Haan, "Livelihoods and Poverty: The Role of Migration – A Critical Review of the Migration Literature" *Journal of Development Studies* 36(2) (1999): 1-47.

97 Ronald Skeldon, "Rural-Urban Migration and its Implications for Poverty Alleviation" *Asia-Pacific Population Journal* 12(1) (1997): 3-16.

98 de Haan, "Livelihoods and Poverty."

99   Laure-Hélène Piron with Alison Evans, *Politics and the PRSP Approach: Synthesis Paper* Overseas Development Institute, PRSP Monitoring and Synthesis Project, Working Paper No. 237, London, 2004, p.3.

100   Sally Peberdy and John Oucho, *Migration and Poverty in Southern Africa*, Paper for Southern African Migration Project, 2001.

101   de Haan, *Livelihoods and Poverty*; Uma Kothari, *Migration and Chronic Poverty*, Institute for Public and Development Management, Chronic Poverty Research Centre Working Paper 16, University of Manchester, 2002.

102   Skeldon, "Rural-Urban Migration and its Implications for Poverty Alleviation"; Ronald Skeldon, "Migration and Poverty" *Asia-Pacific Population Journal* 17(4) (2002): 67-82.

103   Pierre Fallavier, Chileshe Mulenga and Harrington Jere, "Poverty and Vulnerability Assessment – Zambia: Overview of Shocks and Responses in Low-Income Urban Settlements" Paper prepared for PVA Consultation Workshop, 1-2 March 2005, Lusaka, p.11.

104   Gabriel Demombynes, "A Poverty Profile for Zambia Based on the 2002-03 Living Conditions Monitoring Survey" Paper prepared for PVA Consultation Workshop, 1-2 March 2005, Lusaka, p.38.

105   Barbara Parker and Faustin Mwape, "Poverty and Vulnerability in Zambia, 2004: A Qualitative Study" Background Paper prepared for PVA Consultation Workshop, 1-2 March 2005, Lusaka, p.24.

106   Central Statistical Office (CSO), Government of the Republic of Zambia, *Zambia 2000 Census of Population and Housing, Zambia Analytical Report Vol.10* (Lusaka: CSO, 2003).

107   James Thurlow and Peter Wobst, "The Road to Pro-Poor Growth in Zambia" Paper presented at the DPRU, TIPS and Cornell University Conference on "African Development and Poverty Reduction: The Macro-Micro Linkage", Lord Charles Hotel, Somerset West, Cape Town, 13-15 October 2004, p.39.

108   Parker and Mwape, "Poverty and Vulnerability in Zambia", p.25.

109   Tango International, *Underlying Causes of Livelihood Insecurity among the Poor in Malawi: The Testing of Five Potential Hypotheses* (CARE Southern and Western Africa Regional Management Unit (SWARMU), 2003).

110   Deborah Fahy Bryceson, Jodie Fonseca and John Kadzandira, *Social Pathways from the HIV/AIDS Deadlock of Disease, Denial and Desperation in Rural Malawi* (CARE Malawi, 2004).

111   Timothy Frankenberger, Kristina Luther, Karen Fox and John Mazzeo, *Livelihood Erosion Through Time: Macro and Micro Factors that Influenced Livelihood Trends in Malawi Over the Last 30 Years* (CARE Southern and Western Africa Regional Management Unit, 2003).

112   Christopher Cramer and Nicola Pontara, "Rural Poverty and Poverty Alleviation in Mozambique: What's Missing from the Debate?" *Journal of Modern African Studies* 36(1) (1998): 101-38.

113   Government of Mozambique *Estratégia para a Redução da Pobreza em Moçambique*, (Maputo: Ministério do Plano e Finanças, Government of Mozambique (GOM), 1995) *Mozambique: Rural Poverty Profile* (Maputo: Ministério do Plano e Finanças. Poverty Alleviation Unit, 1996).

114   Gibbon, "The African Growth Opportunities Act"; Lall, "FDI, AGOA and Manufactured Exports".

115   Stephen Turner, *The Southern African Crisis: Lesotho Literature Review* (Care International, 2003).

116   Alison Evans with Erin Coyle and Zaza Curran, *National Poverty Reduction Strategies (PRSPs) in Conflict-Affected Countries in Africa*. Overseas Development Institute, PRSP Monitoring & Synthesis Project Briefing Note No. 6, London, 2003.

117   United Republic of Tanzania, *Poverty Reduction Strategy Paper (PRSP)* (Dar es Salaam: Government Printer, 2000).

118   United Republic of Tanzania, *Draft Poverty Reduction Strategy Paper II* (Dar es Salaam, 2004).

119   Republic of Mozambique, *Action Plan for the Reduction of Absolute Poverty (2001-05) (PARPA)* (Maputo, 2001).

120   Republic of Zambia, *Zambia: Poverty Reduction Strategy Paper: 2002 – 2004* (Lusaka: Ministry of Finance and National Planning, 2002).

121   Government of Malawi, *Malawi Poverty Reduction Strategy Paper* (Lilongwe: Government Press, 2002).

122   Kingdom of Lesotho, *Poverty Reduction Strategy 2004/2005 – 2006/2007* (Maseru: Government Printers, 2005).

123   Turner, *The Southern African Crisis*, p.34.

124   Republic of Zambia, *Zambia: Poverty Reduction Strategy Paper*, pp.82-3.

125   Government of Malawi, *Malawi Poverty Reduction Strategy Paper*, p.86.

126   Sechaba Consultants, *Riding the Tiger: Lesotho Miners and Attitudes Towards Permanent Residence in South Africa*, SAMP Migration Policy Series No.2, 1997, p.vi.

127   Government of Malawi, *Malawi Poverty Reduction Strategy Paper*, p.75.

128   Gary Kynoch and Theresa Ulicki, *Cross-Border Raiding and Community Conflict in the Lesotho-South Africa Border Zone*, SAMP Migration Policy Series No. 21, 2001.

129   Ibid; Turner, *The Southern African Crisis*; Stephen Turner with Rebecca Calder, John Gay, David Hall, Jane Iredale, Clare Mbizule and 'Mamohau Mohatla, *Livelihoods in Lesotho* (Maseru: CARE Lesotho, 2001); T. Leboela and Stephen Turner, *The Voice of the People: Report on Community Consultations for the National Vision and the Poverty Reduction Strategy Paper* (Maseru: 2002).

130   Kingdom of Lesotho, *Poverty Reduction Strategy 2004/2005 – 2006/2007*, p.37.

131   United Republic of Tanzania, *Draft Poverty Reduction Strategy Paper II*.

132   Government of Malawi, *Malawi Poverty Reduction Strategy Paper*, p.58.

133   Kingdom of Lesotho, *Poverty Reduction Strategy 2004/2005 – 2006/2007*, p.73.

134   Ibid.

135   Rachel Sabates-Wheeler and Myrthe Waite, *Migration and Social Protection: A Concept Paper*, Development Research Centre on Migration, Globalisation and Poverty Working Paper T2, University of Sussex, Brighton, 2003.

136   Government of Malawi, *Malawi Poverty Reduction Strategy Paper*, p.68.

137   C. Gannon, K. Gwilliam, Z. Liu and C. Malmberg-Calvo, "Transport" In Jeni Klugman (ed.) *A Sourcebook for Poverty Reduction Strategies, Volume 2: Macroeconomic and Sectoral Approaches* (Washington, D.C.: World Bank, 2002), p.330.

138   Republic of Mozambique, *Action Plan for the Reduction of Absolute Poverty*, p.4.

139   Republic of Zambia, *Zambia: Poverty Reduction Strategy Paper*, p.103.

140   Government of Malawi, *Malawi Poverty Reduction Strategy Paper*, pp.40-41.

141   World Bank, *Toward a Conflict-Sensitive Poverty Reduction Strategy: Lessons from a Retrospective Analysis* (Washington, D.C.: World Bank, 2005), p.12.

142   Republic of Angola, *Estratégia de Combate à Pobreza Reinserção Social, Reabilitação e Reconstrução e Estabilização Económica*, (Ministério do Planeamento, Direcção de Estudos e Planeamento, 2004).

143   Democratic Republic of the Congo, *Interim Poverty Reduction Strategy Paper* (Kinshasa, 2002).

144   Evans et al, *National Poverty Reduction Strategies (PRSPs) in Conflict-Affected Countries in Africa*, p.13.

145   Democratic Republic of the Congo, *Interim Poverty Reduction Strategy Paper*.

146   Democratic Republic of the Congo, *Second Progress Report on the I-PRSP Implementation and the Formulation of the Full PRSP June 2003-June 2004* (Kinshasa: Ministry of Planning, 2004).

147   Global IDP Project, *Internal Displacement: Global Overview of Trends and Developments in 2004* (Geneva, Switzerland: Global IDP Project, Norwegian Refugee Council, 2005).

148   United Nations High Commissioner for Refugees, *Poverty Reduction Strategy Papers – A Displacement Perspective* (Geneva: UNHCR, 2004).

149   United Republic of Tanzania, *Poverty Reduction Strategy Paper (PRSP)*.

150   United Republic of Tanzania, *Draft Poverty Reduction Strategy Paper II*.

151   Democratic Republic of the Congo, *Interim Poverty Reduction Strategy Paper*, p.14.

152   IMF and World Bank, *Poverty Reduction Strategy Papers – Operational Issues* (Washington, D.C.: International Monetary Fund and World Bank, 1999); Jeni Klugman (ed), *A Sourcebook for Poverty Reduction Strategies* (Washington: World Bank, 2002).

153 H. Alderman, L. Cord, N. Chaudhury, C. Cornelius, N. Okidegbe, C.D. Scott and S. Schonberger, "Rural Poverty", Draft chapter in Jeni Klugman (ed.) *A Sourcebook for Poverty Reduction Strategies, Volume 2: Macroeconomic and Sectoral Approaches* (Washington: World Bank, 2001), p.37.

154 Ibid, p.37.

155 Ibid, p.37.

156 Ibid, p.38.

157 Ibid, p.38.

158 Ibid, pp.14, 37.

159 Klugman, *Sourcebook for Poverty Reduction Strategies, Volume 2*.

160 Ibid, p.127.

161 Ibid.

162 Ibid.

163 Ibid.

164 Ibid, p.234.

165 Ibid, p.255.

166 Ibid, p.181.

167 Ibid, p.337.

168 Ibid, pp.353-54.

169 Ibid, pp.451, 459.

170 Ibid, p.452.

171 Klugman, *Sourcebook for Poverty Reduction Strategies, Volume 1*.

172 Trust Fund for the Social Integration of Vulnerable Groups, *Action Plan for Poverty Alleviation (APPA)* (Mauritius, 2001).

173 Government of the Republic of Namibia, *Poverty Reduction Strategy for Namibia* (Windhoek: National Planning Commission, 1998); Government of the Republic of Namibia, *National Poverty Reduction Action Programme, 2001-2005* (Windhoek: National Planning Commission, 2001); Government of the Republic of Namibia, *Second National Development Plan 2001/2002 – 2005/2006 Volume 1 and 2: Macroeconomic, Sectoral and Cross-Sectoral Policies*, (Windhoek: National Planning Commission, 2002).

174 Republic of South Africa *Growth, Employment and Redistribution: A Macroeconomic Strategy (GEAR)* (Pretoria: Ministry of Finance, 1996).

175 Kingdom of Swaziland, *Draft Poverty Reduction Strategy and Action Plan (PRSAP) Volume I*. (Mbabane: Ministry of Economic Planning and Development, 2005); Kingdom of Swaziland, *Draft Action Programmes for the Reduction of Poverty, PRSAP Vol. II* (Mbabane: Ministry of Economic Planning and Development, 2005).

176   Michael Aliber, "Chronic Poverty in South Africa: Incidence, Causes and Policies" *World Development*, 31(3) (2003): 473-90.

177   African National Congress (ANC), *Reconstruction and Development Programme: A Policy Framework* (Johannesburg: Umanyano Press, 1994).

178   Republic of South Africa, *White Paper on Reconstruction and Development* (Pretoria: Government Printer, 1994). Henceforth, the terms RDP Base Document and RDP White Paper will be used to differentiate between the two policy documents.

179   Doreen Atkinson and Lochner Marais, "Urbanisation and the Future Urban Agenda in South Africa" In Udesh Pillay, Richard Tomlinson and Jacques du Toit (eds.) *Democracy and Delivery: Urban Policy in South Africa* (Cape Town: HSRC Press, 2006), pp.22-49.

180   ANC, *Reconstruction and Development Programme*, p.75.

181   Ibid, p.25.

182   Ibid, p.77.

183   Ibid, p.101.

184   Ibid, p.83.

185   Ibid, p.86.

186   Ibid.

187   Ibid, pp.11, 116-17.

188   Hein Marais, *South Africa: Limits to Change: The Political Economy of Transformation* (Cape Town: UCT Press and Zed Books, 1998); Aliber, "Chronic Poverty in South Africa."

189   Republic of South Africa, *Growth, Employment and Redistribution*.

190   John Weeks, "Stuck in Low Gear? Macroeconomic Policy in South Africa, 1996-1998" *Cambridge Journal of Economics* 23 (2001): 795-811.

191   Jonathan Michie and Vishnu Padayachee, "Three Years after Apartheid: Growth, Employment and Redistribution?" *Cambridge Journal of Economics* 22 (1998): 623-35.

192   Judith Streak, "The Gear Legacy: Did Gear Fail or Move South Africa Forward in Development?" *Development Southern Africa* 21(2) (2004): 271-88.

193   Republic of South Africa, *Growth, Employment and Redistribution*, p. A-35

194   Republic of South Africa, *Integrated Sustainable Rural Development Strategy* (Pretoria, 2000).

195   Thabo Mbeki, "The State of the Nation Address of the President of South Africa" at the National Assembly Chamber, Cape Town, 9 February 2001.

196   Atkinson and Marais, *Urbanisation and the Future Urban Agenda in South Africa*; Development Bank of South Africa (DBSA), *Development Report 2005 – Overcoming Underdevelopment in South Africa's Second Economy* (Midrand: DBSA, 2005).

197   DBSA, *Development Report 2005*, p.56.

198   RSA, *Integrated Sustainable Rural Development Strategy*, p.8.

199   Mark Oranje, "The Integrated Sustainable Rural Development Programme (ISRDP): Critiques, Easy Answers and the Really Difficult Questions" Paper presented at the joint UNDP, HSRC and DBSA Conference on Overcoming Underdevelopment in South Africa's Second Economy, 28-29 October 2004, Sheraton Hotel, Pretoria; DBSA, *Development Report 2005*.

200   Ibid, p.14.

201   In this regard, the ISRDP states that 'with a more active land reform, however, growing tourism, and responsive programmes of public investment, rural youth in areas of low potential will see new opportunities in more dynamic rural areas and small towns' (Republic of South Africa, *Integrated Sustainable Rural Development Strategy*, p.21).

202   DBSA, *Development Report 2005*, p.58.

203   Policy Co-ordination and Advisory Services, The Presidency Republic of South Africa (PCAS) *National Spatial Development Perspective* (Pretoria, 2003); Atkinson and Marais, *Urbanisation and the Future Urban Agenda in South Africa*, p.22.

204   Oranje, *Integrated Sustainable Rural Development Programme*, p.14.

205   Atkinson and Marais, *Urbanisation and the Future Urban Agenda in South Africa*, pp.23-4. In contrast with what they view as the rather nebulous, rhetorical policy statements that preceeded it.

206   Ibid.

207   Policy Co-ordination and Advisory Services, The Presidency, Republic of South Africa (PCAS), and the Department of Provincial and Local Government (DPLG) *Provincial Growth and Development Strategy Guidelines* (Pretoria, 2005) p.1.

208   Ibid, p.2.

209   Ibid, p.3.

210   Province of the Eastern Cape, *Strategy Framework for Growth and Development 2004-2014*, pp.9-10.

211   Ibid, p.7.

212   Ibid, p.12.

213   Provincial Government: Western Cape, *Development and Growth Through Equity: Provincial Growth and Development Strategy*, pp.2-3.

214   Ibid, pp.4-5.

215   Ibid, p.3.

216   Ibid, p.4.

217   Ibid, p.11.

218   Ibid, p.16.

219   Ibid, p.23.

220   Gauteng Provincial Government, *A Growth & Development Strategy (GDS) for the Gauteng Province*, April 2005.

221   Ibid, p.9.

222   Ibid, p.11.

223   Ibid, p.15.

224   Ibid, p.31.

225   Philip Harrison, "The Genealogy of South Africa's Integrated Development Plan" *Third World Planning Review* 23(2) (2001): 175-93.

226   Ibid.

227   Alison Todes, "Regional Planning and Sustainability: Reshaping Development through Integrated Development Plans in the Ugu District of South Africa" Paper presented to the Regional Studies Association Conference, Reinventing Regions in the Global Economy, Pisa, 12-15 April 2003.

228   Ibid, and Philip Harrison, *Towards Integrated Inter-Governmental Planning in South Africa: the IDP as a Building Block*, Report to the Department of Provincial and Local Government and Municipal Demarcation Board, 2002.

229   City of Johannesburg, *Integrated Development Plan 2004/05*, p.29.

230   Ibid, p.29.

231   Ibid, p.36.

232   Ibid, chapter 5.

233   Ibid, p.69.

234   Ibid, p.72.

235   Ibid, p.75.

236   Ibid, pp.183, 214, 267.

237   Ibid, p.317.

238   City of Tshwane, *Tshwane IDP 2004*, Revision cycle no. 2. August 2004.

239   Ibid, p.65.

240   Ibid, pp.67-68.

241   Ibid, pp.63, 80.

242   Ibid, p.262.

243   Ibid.

244   Ibid, p.477.

245   Ibid, pp.491, 569, 623, 665.

246   Ekurhuleni Municipality, *IDP Review*. June 2004.

247   City of Cape Town *Draft Integrated Development Plan 2004/2005*. March 2004; City of Cape Town, *Integrated Development Plan 2005/2006*.

248   City of Cape Town, *Draft Integrated Development Plan 2004/2005*, pp.18-19.

249   Ibid, p.18.

250   Ibid, pp.44-46.

251   City of Cape Town, *Integrated Development Plan 2005/2006*, pp.11-12.

252   Ibid, pp.11-12.

253   Ibid, pp.40, 75.

254   eThekwini Municipality, *Integrated Development Plan 2003-2007* (June 2003).

255   eThekwini Municipality, *The Reviewed Integrated Development Plan 2003-2007* (June 2004)

256   Ibid, p.37.

257   Nelson Mandela Metropolitan Municipality, *Integrated Development Plan* (2002-2006).

258   Ibid, p.54.

259   Ibid, p.61.

260   Ibid, p.150.

261   Ibid, pp.1069-1076; Bruce Frayne and Wade Pendleton, *Mobile Namibia: Migration Trends and Attitudes*, SAMP Migration Policy Series No. 27, 2002, pp.10-13.

262   Frayne and Pendleton, "Migration in Namibia", pp.1075-76.

263   Ibid, p.1056.

264   Government of the Republic of Namibia, *Poverty Reduction Strategy for Namibia*, p.5.

265   Government of the Republic of Namibia, *National Poverty Reduction Action Programme, 2001-2005*, p.18.

266   GRN, *Poverty Reduction Strategy for Namibia*, p.1.

267   Ibid., p.6.

268   Ibid.

269   GRN, *National Poverty Reduction Action Programme, 2001-2005*, p.20.

270   Ibid, p.19.

271   Frayne and Pendleton, "Migration in Namibia", p.1072.

272   GRN, *National Poverty Reduction Action Programme, 2001-2005*, p.22.

273 Ibid., p.32.

274 Oladele Arowolo, "Namibia's Population Policy" In Ben Fuller and Isolde Prommer (eds.), *Population–Development–Environment in Namibia: Background Readings* (Windhoek: Multidisciplinary Research and Consultancy Centre, University of Namibia, 2000), p.248.

275 Government of the Republic of Namibia, *Second National Development Plan 2001/2002 – 2005/2006. Volume 1 and 2*, pp.36-37.

276 Hamilton Simelane and Jonathan Crush, *Swaziland Moves: Perceptions and Patterns of Modern Migration*, SAMP Migration Policy Series No. 32, 2004.

277 Ibid.

278 Kingdom of Swaziland, *Draft Poverty Reduction Strategy and Action Plan (PRSAP) Volume I*. Kingdom of Swaziland, *Draft Action Programmes for the Reduction of Poverty, PRSAP Vol. II*.

279 Kingdom of Swaziland, *Draft Poverty Reduction Strategy and Action Plan (PRSAP) Volume I*, p.20.

280 Ibid, pp.151-2.

281 Ibid, p.156.

282 Ibid, p.35.

283 Kingdom of Swaziland, *Draft Action Programmes for the Reduction of Poverty, PRSAP Vol. II*, pp.49, 66.

284 Kingdom of Swaziland, *Draft Poverty Reduction Strategy and Action Plan (PRSAP) Volume I*, p.129

285 UNAIDS, *2004 Report on the Global AIDS Epidemic*.

286 David Wilson, *Lesotho and Swaziland: HIV/AIDS Risk Assessment at Cross-Border and Migrant Sites in Southern Africa* (Arlington: FHI, 2001); Brian Williams, Eleanor Gouws, Mark Lurie and Jonathan Crush, *Spaces of Vulnerability: Migration and HIV/AIDS in South Africa*, SAMP Migration Policy Series No. 24, 2002.

287 Kingdom of Swaziland, *Draft Poverty Reduction Strategy and Action Plan (PRSAP) Volume I*, p.103.

288 Simelane and Crush, *Swaziland Moves*.

289 Ibid, p.48-49.

290 Kingdom of Swaziland, *Draft Action Programmes for the Reduction of Poverty, PRSAP Vol. II*, p.94.

291 Kingdom of Swaziland, *Draft Poverty Reduction Strategy and Action Plan (PRSAP) Volume I*, pp.153-4.

292 Ibid, p.71.

293 Simelane and Crush, *Swaziland Moves*.

294   Kingdom of Swaziland, *Poverty Reduction Strategy and Action Plan (PRSAP) Volume I*, p.49

295   Black, *Migration and Pro-Poor Policies in Africa*.

296   Nigel Harris, "Migration and Development" *Economic & Political Weekly* 43(40) (2005).

297   Ibid.

298   de Haan, "Livelihoods and Poverty"; Kothari, *Migration and Chronic Poverty*; Skeldon, "Migration and Poverty"; Hugh Waddington and Rachel Sabates-Wheeler, *How Does Poverty Affect Migration Choice? A Review of Literature*, Institute of Development Studies, Development Research Centre on Migration, Globalisation and Poverty Working Paper T3, University of Sussex, 2003; Frank Ellis and Nigel Harris, "New Thinking About Urban and Rural Development", Keynote Paper for DFID Sustainable Development Retreat, University of Surrey, Guildford, 13 July 2004.

299   Maxwell, "Heaven or Hubris".

300   See for example the SADC presentations to the High Level Dialogue on Migration and Development, http://www.queensu.ca/samp/migrationnews/HLD_statements. htm.

301   http://www.queensu.ca/samp/midsa/.

302   Oucho, *Cross-Border Migration and Regional Initiatives in Managing Migration in Southern Africa*.

303   Ibid; Crush, Williams and Peberdy, "Migration in Southern Africa."

304   Naila Kabeer, *Gender Mainstreaming in Poverty Eradication and the Millennium Development Goals: A Handbook for Policy-Makers and Other Stakeholders* (London: Commonwealth Secretariat, 2003), p.205.

305   International Development Committee, *Migration and Development*.

306   ANC, *Reconstruction and Development Programme*; RSA, *White Paper on Reconstruction and Development*.

307   Republic of South Africa, *Growth, Employment and Redistribution*.

308   South African Cities Network (SACN), *State of the Cities Report 2004* (Johannesburg: South African Cities Network, 2004); Catherine Cross, Pieter Kok, Marie Wentzel, Kholadi Tlabela, Gina Weir-Smith and John Mafukidze, *Poverty Pockets in Gauteng: How Migration Impacts Poverty. Report to the Gauteng Intersectoral Development Unit* (Pretoria: Human Sciences Research Council, 2005).

309   International Organisation for Migration (IOM). *World Migration 2005: Costs and Benefits of International Migration* (Geneva: IOM, 2005), p.259.

310   Priya Deshingkar and Edward Anderson, *People on the Move: New Policy Challenges for Increasingly Mobile Populations*, Overseas Development Institute, Natural Resource Perspectives No. 92, London, 2004.

311   Priya Deshingkar and Daniel Start, *Seasonal Migration for Livelihoods in India: Coping, Accumulation and Exclusion.* Overseas Development Institute, Working Paper 220, London, 2003; Priya Deshingkar, *Seasonal Migration; How Rural is Rural?* Overseas Development Institute, ODI Opinions No. 52, London, 2005.

312   Department for International Development (DFID), *Migration and Pro-Poor Policy in Sub-Saharan Africa: Summary of Key Findings*, DFID Policy Brief, London 2004; Department for International Development (DFID), *Mainstreaming Migration in Southern Africa: Summary of Key Findings*, DFID Policy Brief, London, 2004.

313   DFID, *Mainstreaming Migration in Southern Africa.*

314   S. Ammassari, *Migration and Development: New Strategic Outlooks and Practical Ways Forward: The Cases of Angola and Zambia*, IOM Migration Research Series, No. 5, Geneva, 2005; Crush, Williams and Peberdy, "Migration in Southern Africa."

315   PCAS and DPLG, *Provincial Growth and Development Strategy Guidelines*, p.5.

316   Harrison, "The genealogy of South Africa's Integrated Development Plan"; Tony Binns and Etienne Nel, "Supporting Local Economic Development in Post-Apartheid South Africa" *Local Economy* 17(1) (2002): 8-24.

Appendix 1: The Coverage of Migration in Poverty Reduction Strategies in Southern Africa

Country	Poverty Diagnostics	Priority Public Actions
Post-Conflict Countries		
Democratic Republic of Congo (D.R.C.) *Interim Poverty Reduction Strategy (Mar 2002)*	• The economic, social, political, and environmental costs of this conflict have been huge. More than three million human lives have been lost. Almost four million people are estimated to have been displaced in the sub-region and some 10,000 to 15,000 children are being used as soldiers. The extent and complexity of the conflict have seriously undermined institutional stability and eroded grassroots socio-economic infrastructure. • Malnutrition is a major public health problem. In November 2000, the World Food Program (WFP) calculated that 16 million people (33 percent of the population) suffered from serious malnutrition following prolonged displacement, isolation, lack of access to markets, disruption of supply routes, and inflation	The intermediate strategies that could allow the DRC to achieve its stated objective are based on 3 pillars, namely: • Peace and good governance; • Stabilization and pro-poor growth; and • Community dynamics. The migration related content of the I-PRSP strategies is found predominantly under the first of these pillars, as outlined below. **Pillar I: Peace and Good Governance** **Axis 1: Restore and consolidate internal peace** To achieve lasting peace, the government has committed itself, between 2002 and 2005, to (inter alia): • Reunite families, above all by bringing back children and other people displaced by the fighting; • Continue the demobilization and reintegration of child soldiers;

Country	Poverty Diagnostics	Priority Public Actions
Democratic Republic of Congo (D.R.C.) *Interim Poverty Reduction Strategy (Mar 2002)*	• Environment: In the eastern part of the country, natural ecosystems are under intense and devastating pressure. The influx of 2 million refugees from Rwanda and Burundi in 1994, in the wake of the crisis in those two countries, led to deforestation and the destruction of fauna in the wildlife parks. • Gender-based violence: sexual violence has been inflicted upon women by armed combatants, especially those from foreign armies coming from countries with a very high incidence of HIV/AIDS. • Urban poverty: The crisis that has engulfed the DRC since the 1970s, the failure of the stabilization and structural adjustment programs of the 1980s, the plundering of the country twice during the 1990s, and the wars of 1996 and 1998 induced massive displacements of people to the big towns and thereby altered the patterns of urban poverty. In twelve recently surveyed provinces, urban poverty is estimated at 75 percent. The once richest towns in the country, especially Kinshasa and Lubumbashi, are currently poorer than Mbuji-Mayi, Boma and Matadi. • In the eastern part of the country, war has aggravated the poverty of both the displaced population and the local host communities. Much more of an emphasis is placed on the impact of the conflict on basic infrastructure.	**Axis 2: Address the needs of the victims of the fighting** There is a basically reciprocal relation between conflicts and poverty. Poverty generates conflicts, which, in turn, exacerbate the destitution of the victims of those conflicts: loss of human life, mass displacements of the population, material destruction, deterioration of infrastructure, and disruption of socio-economic circuits. This situation has plunged a sizeable percentage of the population into poverty and destitution so severe that emergency measures are needed. The government has taken two kinds of measures with respect to demobilization and reinsertion into civilian life (Decree-Law No. 0066 of June 9, 2000). To combat poverty exacerbated by wars and conflicts, the government is contemplating implementing a post-conflict program for reconstruction and economic recovery, both of which are essential to the peace process. • Care for the victims of ethnic and regional conflicts in the country Problems: The conflicts, in turn, have plunged the civil and military population into poverty and destitution. They have brought loss of human life, mass displacements of the population, enrolment of children in the army, material destruction, and damage to infrastructure Objectives: Care for the victims of conflicts and expedite the process of demobilization of child soldiers and reinsertion of the population into normal life Priority actions: - Demobilization and disarmament of combatants and child soldiers - Preparation of a post-conflict program for the supervision and psychological, socioeconomic and medical rehabilitation of the victims. Efforts should focus on education, health and housing - Reuniting of families and relocation of displaced communities and refugees

Country	Poverty Diagnostics	Priority Public Actions
Angola	Successive armed conflict produced an enormous displacement of the population, resulting in an influx of people from rural areas into provincial capitals and from the interior into cities along the coast. Approximately 4 million Angolans (30% of the population) were displaced from their traditional areas of residence and economic activities. In 2003, after a year of peace, it was estimated that more than a million *deslocados* (internally displaced) had returned to their areas of origin, with a further 2,2m internally displaced persons, 450,000 refugees in neighbouring countries, 85,000 demobilised Unita soldiers and 360,000 dependants needing to be reintegrated into society. **Consequences:** Forced migration resulted in unsustainable urbanisation processes, the effects including: • The sudden impoverishment of the displaced population, many of them living in urban and suburban areas. Urban poverty, estimated at 61% in 1995, has been exacerbated by the influx of *deslocados* to the cities. • Pressure on existing urban social infrastructure, resulting in the rapid destruction of physical assets and low basic service maintenance. The inadequate supply of accommodation has produced a burgeoning periphery, with high density rates, the accumulation of refuse, non-existent sanitation and potable water, and high rates of unemployment and underemployment. Some cities and provincial capitals in the interior have been affected by regular disruptions to the electricity supply; damaged potable water supply systems; deteriorating public education and health services; industrial decline due to the destruction and damaging of machinery and physical infrastructure and the loss of the technical elite; destruction of formal urban and rural commerce. • Pressure on existing job availability, with a rapid expansion of the informal sector;	• Progress indicators: - Combatants and child soldiers demobilized and disarmed - Post-conflict programme drawn up: victims of conflicts rehabilitated and reinserted into normal life • Social reinsertion: strategy supporting the movement of returnees, refugees, demobilised and their dependant families to their areas of origin or resettlement areas and supporting their reintegration by promoting productive activities and installing basic social services. • Security and civil protection: clearance of mines to help facilitate the free movement of people and goods, especially in rural areas which were adversely affected by the armed conflict and are a main destination of the displaced • Food Security and rural development: Only mentions that the limited social infrastructure that exists to support returning displaced families remains a constraint to the expansion of the rural sector. • HIV/AIDS: Although the HIV prevalence rate was estimated as 5.7% in 2001, with the increase in the free movement of people following the 2002 peace accord, due to the opening of roads, the return of refugees and the opening of borders with neighbouring countries, there is a real concern about the spread of HIV/AIDS. The main target groups of intervention include youth, adults with high mobility (truck drivers, military personnel), PLWAs and their families and AIDS orphans. Interventions include preventative measures, extending access to primary health care, and improving the nutrition of PLWAs. • Education: Adult literacy programme, giving special attention to women, as well as those demobilised and displaced by the war.

Country	Poverty Diagnostics	Priority Public Actions
	• Social fragmentation due to the absence or poor functioning of social security mechanisms, resulting in a notable increase in phenomena such as street children; • Increasing unemployment and under-employment in urban areas. **Main causes of poverty include:** • Armed conflict: resulted in displacement of the population, the destruction of traditional economic activities, social infrastructure and means of communication, and disruption in the distribution of products and other essential goods. • Strong demographic pressure, due to high fertility rates, high dependency ratios and the massive migration movements towards the big cities.	• Health: Again, mention is made of the potential rise in the transmission of HIV with the increasing migratory flows. The health sector programme aims to improve the health status of Angolan citizens without discrimination and based on equity principles. It is particularly concerned with poor and vulnerable groups living in areas recently accessible, in resettlement zones and those strongly affected by war. • Basic infrastructure: The improvement of road networks are seen as fundamental for ensuring better access to markets and facilitating mobility, especially for the rural population which is dependent on agriculture. The Basic Infrastructure Reconstruction and Rehabilitation Programme aims in the first phase to (i) establish the circulation of people and goods inside Angola; (ii) make the return of displaced people to their zones of origin possible; (iii) facilitate the transportation of agricultural produce to markets; (iv) rapidly create jobs for demobilised soldiers. The second phase of the programme focuses on: (v) improving conditions for the movement of people and goods; and (vi) reducing high transport costs. Special attention will be paid to measures of preventing HIV/AIDS, as demobilised soldiers, who are being targeted for road repairs and other forms of public works, have a relatively high rate of infection. In terms of housing, the aim is to guarantee that all Angolan families have adequate housing conditions, including resettled and internally displaced people. • Employment and professional formation: this programme is targeted at vulnerable groups, including women, displaced people and the disabled. • Governance: no mention of mobile populations. • Macroeconomic management: no mention of mobile populations.

Country	Poverty Diagnostics	Priority Public Actions
Low Income Countries		
Tanzania (PRSP I, Oct 2000) (Draft PRSP II, Aug 2004)	Under *The Status of Poverty in Tanzania*: 'A major concern of the poor is their vulnerability to unpredictable events. In Tanzania, famine often results from either floods or drought. Since the mid-1990s, Tanzania has in fact experienced a series of adverse weather conditions, which undermined food security. Another threat is the increasing impact of HIV/AIDS on the number of orphans, currently estimated at 680,000. Many communities have to deal with growing numbers of AIDS victims and orphans, the handicapped, the very old, and refugees. There is, therefore, a growing need for safety-nets' (PRSP I, p.9) Note: in the draft PRSP II, vulnerable groups are identified as 'children, persons with disabilities, youths (unemployed, youths with unreliable income and female youths), elderly persons, people living with long illness and HIV and AIDS, women (widows, other women who are not able to support themselves) and drug addicts and alcoholics (draft PRSP II, pp.7-8). Refugees have fallen away as a vulnerable group. These groups were determined by a PPA conducted in 2002.	Under *The Strategy for Poverty Reduction – Rural Sector Development and Export Growth*: 'Rationalizing physical controls that constrain crop movements within the country and across international borders' (PRSP I, p.17) Under *Improvement of quality of life and social well-being*: 'The government recognizes the slow pace of ensuring better town planning and improvement of quality housing in rural areas. The supply of new houses in urban areas is outstripped by massive rural-urban migration, and where such housing is available, it is of low quality, is in a poor environment, and has inadequate or no access to essential utilities of clean water, electricity, roads and sewerage lines. Most of the settlements are un-serviced. Adequate sanitation and sustainable access to safe and clean water and shelter play a critical role in supporting livelihoods and ensuring health. Measures to this effect will be taken to ensure improved access and quality of such services' (draft PRSP II, p.32)

Country	Poverty Diagnostics	Priority Public Actions
Mozambique	Under *Strategic Vision for Poverty Reduction Mozambique*: 'A fundamental role of the State in stimulating a market economy and expanding opportunities for the poor lies in the development of basic infrastructure. Improvements in the road network will permit better access to markets and a reduction in costs, and will facilitate communication and mobility, especially for those who live in rural areas and depend on agriculture. In parallel, the provision of water and energy is fundamental to the development of human capital and the expansion of national output. Priority in the rehabilitation and construction of basic infrastructure will be given to those areas of the country with the largest populations and highest levels of poverty' (p.4) Under *Characteristics of Poverty: Concepts and Perceptions*: 'With regard to **causes [of poverty]**, in the 1996 assessments there was frequent reference to the war as a determining factor in explaining the current conditions of the poorest segments of the population. Ignorance and adverse climatic conditions were also considered to be causes of poverty. In the most recent diagnoses, less emphasis is given to the war, and more reference is made to the lack of support (social support, support from the Government and other institutions), the lack of employment opportunities, limited access to financial services, problems with marketing, or inability (due to physical or mental factors) to work, as the principal causes of poverty. The phenomenon of displacement (a result of the war) and the closing of factories were also highlighted. The latter was particularly raised in areas where employment in factories was until recently the major source of cash income' (pp.12-13).	Under *Fundamental Areas of Action*: 'The availability of adequate infrastructure (in particular, roads, energy and water) is another basic factor to facilitate the initiatives and actions of citizens and their institutions. Amongst other considerations, infrastructure contributes to the availability and mobility of factors of production, makes possible the process of work, innovation and structural change needed in the medium and long-term, and ensures the functioning and expansion of markets' (pp.40-41) Under *Annex 1: Involvement of partners and civil society organizations in the process of developing the PARPA*: 'Due to the floods, the year 2000 was particularly prodigious in meetings between Government and civil society, with the objective of developing strategies to resettle the displaced population who were victims of the rains' (p.vii).

Country	Poverty Diagnostics	Priority Public Actions
Mozambique	Under *The Territorial Context*: 'Mozambique has one of the lowest urbanisation rates in the world. This means that there is an inevitable tendency for migration to urban areas, and great pressure on the non-agricultural job market in the near future' (p.35) 'Maputo is tied to the zone of influence of the largest economic and industrial zone in Southern Africa, namely Johannesburg. Its growth dynamic is also largely a reflection of the South African dynamic. To these differences may be added the inflow of migrants displaced by the war. All together, this has resulted in a process of cumulative concentration of factors, which serve to accelerate the development of this area in a way that differs from the rest of the country' (p.35)	
Zambia (Mar 2002)	No mention of migration related issues	Under *Health – Situation Analysis*: 'there is a growing recognition in Zambia of the two-way link between HIV/AIDS and poverty. HIV/AIDS is inexorably consuming more resources, which means that less are available for other life threatening diseases such as malaria and cholera. Another threat in some districts is refugee arrivals from neighbouring countries. It is estimated that in one of the country's provinces around 127,000 refugees from a neighbouring country have spontaneously settled in various districts. Where the base populations are quite small, such an influx can have a significant impact on the resources available and the demands generated' (pp.82-83) Under *Transport and Communication – Situation Analysis*: 'The poor state of rural feeder roads inhibits mobility and accessibility. As a result, access to farm inputs and other social amenities and marketing of farm produce are also made very difficult and, thus, deepen poverty in rural areas where the only form of access is by road. Due to lack of transport, a considerable part of the rural population walks long distances to the health centres, schools, and other social amenities' (p.103)

Country	Poverty Diagnostics	Priority Public Actions
Zambia (Mar 2002)		Under *Rural Travel and Transport*: 'In order to improve rural travel and transport, the following measures have been proposed: Facilitate the introduction and promotion of appropriate motorised and non-motorised means of transport aimed at improved mobility in rural areas' (pp.105-106). Under *Cross-Cutting Issues: HIV/AIDS*: 'In order to reduce the number of new HIV cases, the programme will aim to promote safe sex practices among the high-risk groups such as youths, men, sex workers, and prisoners. This will be achieved through several means: Firstly, the implementation of multi-sectoral behaviour change communication campaigns will be effected…Although the programmes are expected to reach all sectors of Zambian society, the priority target groups for these interventions will include youths in the 15-24 age group, and high risk groups including sex workers, military and uniformed personnel, anglers and fish traders, truckers, prisoners, and refugees' (p.110). 'Improve the Quality of Life of Orphans and Vulnerable Children (OVC): The focus will be the expansion of existing programmes, targeting the high-risk groups with peer education, drama, condom promotion/distribution, and other interpersonal outreach activities. There is need to scale up existing programmes that work with high-risk groups, including military and uniformed personnel, prisoners, sex workers, truckers, refugees, and fishermen and fish traders. Support to these projects will be through modest grants of financial assistance to CBOs, FBOs, and other community groups, and assistance that strengthens the capacity of these groups to care for the most vulnerable community members' (p.111).

Country	Poverty Diagnostics	Priority Public Actions
Zambia (Mar 2002)		Under *Poverty Monitoring and Evaluation*: In terms of core PRSP monitoring indicators, one goal is 'to expand, rehabilitate and invest in the road sector so as to improve accessibility and mobility'. The indicator is km of tarred, paved and unpaved road (p.135). Under *Appendix 2-11: Transport and Communications Policy Actions*: 'to expand, rehabilitate and invest in the road sector so as to improve accessibility and mobility and bring a core road network of 33,500 km up to maintainable condition" (p.172-173; p.194)
Malawi	**Poverty Analysis and Profile** Under *Spatial distribution of poverty*: 'The Southern Region has the highest proportion of poor households compared to the other two regions in the country. Using IHS data, 68.1 percent of the population in the Southern Region were poor as compared to 62.8 percent for the Central Region and 62.5 percent for the Northern Region. The Southern Region's poverty situation can partly be explained mainly by migration into the Region and by the small size of cropland holdings per capita' (p.6) **Structural Adjustment and Poverty** Under *Economic Performance during Adjustment*: 'Starting from 1979, Malawi suffered from a series of exogenous shocks, including high import costs due to oil price shocks, disruptions in trade routes, the influx of refugees from Mozambique and droughts that disrupted the pattern of growth. In addition, policy weaknesses and slippages exacerbated the effect of these external shocks. As a result of these internal and external factors, real GDP growth fluctuated between 1979 and 1987' (p.13).	**Pillar 1: Sustainable pro-poor growth** Under *rural infrastructure*: 'Investment in rural roads has direct impact on linking the rural areas, urban and peri-urban areas. Improved access to rural areas reduces transport costs and leads to the creation of marketing networks to enhance value adding. Rural feeder roads also have social benefits through better access to social services such as health centres by facilitating mobility. Further, improved rural infrastructure will alleviate gender disparities, as women bear the burden of transporting heavy loads and travelling long distances to access social services' (p.41) **Pillar 2: Human capital development** - Education - Technical, entrepreneurial vocational education and training - Health Under *Health and Population*: 'A major problem leading to Malawi's poor health indicators is a lack of qualified and adequately compensated medical staff, in terms of doctors, nurses and related personnel. This problem is particularly acute in rural areas, and has been exacerbated by the HIV/AIDS pandemic and internal and external "brain drain" due to low remuneration and poor career prospects' (p58). *Improve Quality of Essential Healthcare*: 'Government will also review the remuneration and career structures for medical staff in order to address problems of attrition through "brain drain"' (p61). - Promotion of good nutrition

Country	Poverty Diagnostics	Priority Public Actions
Malawi		**Pillar 3: Improving the quality of life of the most vulnerable** - Safety nets Under *welfare support interventions*: 'There is a group of people who are unable to fend for themselves and have to rely on others...As a result of over-stretched informal safety nets, some individuals (especially orphans) are forced to move to urban centres to beg and live in unhealthy conditions' (p.68). **Pillar 4: Good governance** - Political will and mindset Under *Security and access to justice*: 'As a result, the rate of crime has risen by 6 percent over the past five years, whilst the crime detection rate has not moved above 20 percent. This has been in part blamed on increases in illegal immigration in the country, which has also contributed to a reduction in economic opportunities for Malawian citizens and has undermined the integrity of Malawian passports' (p.75). **Cross-cutting issues:** Under *HIV/AIDS*: 'in search of income for subsistence and survival, people living in poverty participate in labour migration which results in breakdown of male and female relations, increasing likelihood of multiple sexual partners or casual sexual partners and risk of HIV infection. In addition, women in poverty can be forced to enter into high risk sexual relationship in bartering sex for subsistence. This increases their vulnerability to HIV infection' (p.86).

Country	Poverty Diagnostics	Priority Public Actions
Malawi		Under *Gender and Empowerment:* 'There is a positive relationship between the level of education and movement of social indicators. In Malawi social indicators reveal low education levels among women, with a 44 percent adult literacy rate for women against 72 percent for men. This affects women's access to gainful employment and other economic resources, and further contributes to the poor infant mortality and morbidity rates, high fertility rate, and high HIV infection rate. This emphasizes the need for greater gender equality in education. Full-time female farmers make up 70 percent of the agricultural labour force. However, women continue to have limited access to agricultural extension, training and inputs. This situation is exacerbated by migration of men to towns and estates to seek paid employment, leaving behind low literate women to manage the farms and families. Consequently, over 71 percent of men are in formal employment compared to only 24 percent of women who are mostly concentrated in lowly paid and female-related traditional jobs such as nursing, teaching, home-craft and secretarial jobs' (p.89).

Country	Poverty Diagnostics	Priority Public Actions
Lesotho Draft PRSP (Aug 2004)	Under *Overview*: 'The increase in poor households has been attributed to the highly skewed distribution of wealth, with most of the growth concentrated in the capital; the impact of HIV/AIDS; the massive reduction in remittances from men working in South Africa as a result of mine retrenchments; declining agricultural productivity, due in part to unfavourable climatic conditions; and poor implementation and coordination of development programmes' (p.2) Under *Poverty Diagnosis*: 'For generations the most secure form of income for Basotho has been migrant labour on the mines of South Africa, but with the number of miners now less than half of what they once were, rural households are now struggling to survive. Some households have been able to find work, mostly for younger female members, in the new textile industries. These are, however, concentrated in a few of the urban areas, whereas miners were recruited from all over the country. The availability of waged work makes the urban areas more prosperous, but the influx of job seekers far exceeds the number of positions available. As a result, conditions in the fast-growing peri-urban areas are in decline: services are overwhelmed and the quality of life is in decline' (p.5) 'Throughout the country people spoke of the declining work opportunities that they see as primarily being an outcome of the retrenchment of miners and the destruction of businesses during the unrest of September 1998' (p.6)	Under *Employment Creation and Income Generation – Situation analysis*: 'A rapidly increasing number of households are losing or have lost wage earners as a result of massive retrenchments from the SA mining sector over the past decade and increasingly as the HIV/AIDS pandemic strikes those in their productive years' (p.19) (Potential threats to investment and industrial growth) 'The Government will monitor the implications that rapid employment creation has on migration patterns and the consequences this has for peri-urban infrastructure and housing supply' (p.22) Under *Agriculture and Food Security*: 'Agriculture is often uneconomical while production is inadequate and declining. It is not only Government that has been subsidizing cereal crop production. Over the years households have themselves subsidized ploughing and planting costs by diverting income from other sources – such as mine remittances – to crop production. Because few households keep proper records they are not aware that their costs often exceed their returns' (p.33). 'The impact of mine retrenchments has exacerbated poor production. The decline in mine remittances has had an impact on food production as far fewer households have the necessary income to invest in the required inputs. For poor households the annual hurdle of procuring the required inputs for cereal production is almost insurmountable. In the past this would have been overcome through sharecropping with other households but as the number without wage employment grows, the prospects for sharecropping decline' (pp.33-34)

Country	Poverty Diagnostics	Priority Public Actions
Lesotho Draft PRSP (Aug 2004)	Under *Macroeconomic Framework – structural changes in Lesotho economy:* 'Until the early 1990s, the defining characteristics of Lesotho's dependence on RSA was that nearly 50% of Lesotho's GNI was generated in the form of remittances from Basotho mine-workers employed in South Africa. South Africa remains Lesotho's main trading partner' (p.13) 'The high-LHWP period (1987/88 – 1997/98….The textile and garment industry developed rapidly but employment opportunities for the Basotho in RSA mines started to decline. About two-thirds of GNI was produced locally and remittances comprised only about 36% of GNI' (p.13).	'In border areas there are clear implications of the international dimensions to stock theft that will need to be addressed if any progress is to be made' (p.35) Under *Democracy, Governance, Safety and Security:* 'expanding livestock registration and marking to curb the high rate of livestock theft and sensitizing communities along both sides of the borders about cross-border crime and stock theft' (p.45) Under *Infrastructure Development – Ensure planned settlement of peri-urban areas and affordable access to land:* 'Earlier the Government's concerns regarding the peri-urban areas were noted with regard to utilities. For utility companies to provide a cost-effective service it is important that they should be able to have reasonably easy access to people's homes. The lack of settlement planning in the urban areas prevents this. One reason for the ad hoc pattern of settlement is that acquiring land through proper channels is cumbersome and expensive, leaving the poor with little alternative other than to work through chiefs and field owners' (pp.54-55) Under *Health Care and Social Welfare Analysis – Improve the capacity of health personnel:* 'The government recognizes the enormous contribution made by its health personnel at all levels across the country. In the struggle against HIV/AIDS they are in the front line and deserve to be supported as far as is possible. Specific activities include:…reviewing and improving working conditions of health personnel to address the high rate of staff turnover and brain drain' (p.59).

Country	Poverty Diagnostics	Priority Public Actions
Lesotho Draft PRSP (Aug 2004)		Under *Health Care and Social Welfare Analysis –Revise and update population policy:* 'Lesotho is facing dramatic developments in terms of national population. According to some estimates, the population might have exceeded 3 million by 2015 but, due to the impact of HIV/AIDS, it will only grow to about 2.2 million and it might decline subsequently if no fundamental changes are brought about on a national scale. Coupled with this, migration to the main towns and growth centres (particularly of young people) is likely to continue unabated, throwing many communities in the mountains into decline. For this reason, it is imperative that the Government closely monitors trends and considered the implications. During the three year period a new population policy will be drafted and related to other sectors' (p.61). Under *Improving Public Service Delivery:* 'Lesotho takes great pride in being a sovereign state. At the same time it is recognized that it is part and parcel of a regional economy that has depended on migrant labour for generations. Over the last decade, since the fall of apartheid, the pattern of migration has changed so that today it is not only men who work in South Africa but increasingly women of all ages. According to the 2001 Lesotho Demographic Survey, 14% of males and 4% of females over the age of 15 currently work in South Africa, which is equivalent to approximately 120,000 people. For those seeking legal working in South Africa a passport is critical, for both travel and identification purposes' (p.75)

Country	Poverty Diagnostics	Priority Public Actions
Lesotho Draft PRSP (Aug 2004)		'The inefficient service delivery in the Department of Immigration is caused by a lack of technology, poor management, understaffing, demoralization of staff and a poor working environment. This contributes to a backlog in the processing of passport application forms that has now reached an extreme point. To address this problem, immigration officers, in conjunction with their customers, resort to illegal ways of obtaining the travel documents quickly. The current passports (that are being phased out) are not machine-readable and can easily be tampered with. The introduction of Machine Readable Passports will only address part of the overall inefficiency. To really assist the poor, the Department needs to decentralize this service to district level so as to cut transport and time costs for Basotho living in remote areas' (p.75) 'Quality service with regard to visas and work permits is essential if job creation is to be achieved. A serious dissatisfaction in this area is likely to drive investors and tourist out of Lesotho, thereby increasing poverty. The legal framework that governs issuance of visas and permits is the Aliens Control Act of 1966. The Act states conditions of granting visas or deportation, and it establishes what constitutes a lawful and unlawful presence in Lesotho. This is an obsolete and outdated law with very serious shortfalls and it calls for an urgent review' (p.76). 'Four particular objectives have been identified for the PRSP....improve key services, particularly at the Department of Immigration' (p.76).

Country	Poverty Diagnostics	Priority Public Actions
Lesotho Draft PRSP (Aug 2004)		'Government has taken heed of the concerns of ordinary people whose livelihoods are being impaired by service delivery in this critical area. Particular actions to be taken in the next year include: computerizing the passport issuance system; undertaking stringent supervision to curb corruption; delegation of the Minister's authority to facilitate quick approval; decentralization of functions to offices throughout the country; improvement of human resource capacity and numbers to clear the backlog of applications; training of staff (p.77). Under *Cross-Cutting Issues: HIV/AIDS:* 'As in other countries, certain groups within society are more vulnerable and have an increased risk of infection, including women, young adults, children, migrants and people infected with a sexually infected disease' (p.79) Under *Cross-Cutting Issues: Gender:* 'In comparison to a number of African countries, Lesotho does not suffer from extreme inequality. Indeed it has the rather unusual feature of more girls being educated than boys. This relative advantage has enabled women to compete for employment within the country, while historically the more poorly educated men have sought employment in South Africa' (p.84) 'Historically the labour market has been very distorted from a gender perspective, with migrant labour to the mines being the exclusive domain of men. After the advent of democracy in South Africa in 1994 this started to change; by 2001 one fifth of those Basotho working in South Africa were women. Within the country a new distortion is emerging with the rapidly growing textile industries employing virtually only women. Poorly educated men now find themselves standing before two doors that are effectively shut: mine recruitment has virtually ended, and the textile manufacturing sector has no room for them' (pp.84-85)

Country	Poverty Diagnostics	Priority Public Actions
Lesotho Draft PRSP (Aug 2004)		Under *Cross-Cutting Issues: Child and Youth*: 'Unemployment levels are highest for young people. Overall 18.5 % of the unemployed population are adolescents. Unemployment can be correlated with low educational attainment; although even the completion of secondary education does not guarantee employment. Paradoxically, the high level of adult and youth unemployment may contribute to forms of child labour. For example, often when parents are unable to find gainful employment a young boy of the family is sent to herd animals or a young girl is sent to work as a domestic worker. Because these children are often far from home, they are easily exploited and even abused by their employers...Many young girls drop out of school in order to care for younger siblings after mothers leave home in order to seek employment in urban areas' (p.88).

Appendix 2: The Coverage of Migration in Select South African Integrated Development Plans

City of Johannesburg

Ch. 2: Profile and Development Overview

"This chapter sets out a profile of the City and a high-level development Overview that encompasses urbanisation and migration, socio-economic development, environmental development and service delivery" (p.27)

Urbanisation, migration and demographics. "Great Britain and some European countries were amongst the first countries to become urbanised. Their urbanisation was relatively slow, allowing governments time to plan and provide for the needs of increasing urban populations. The rise of the mega-City (cities with more than 10 million people) in developing countries over the past 20 years, is of concern because of incapacity to increase the provision of housing and basic services at the same pace. According to the 2001 Census, South Africa's population increased by 4.2 million people, to 44.6 million, since 1996. The population in Gauteng alone increased by 1.4 million to 8.8 million in 2001. According to Stats SA, 69% of the people who moved out of Limpopo province, 60% of the people who moved out of KwaZulu Natal, and 57% of the people who moved out of Mpumalanga, moved into Gauteng. The population in the City of Johannesburg increased by more than half a million people between 1996 and 2001...Statistics from the 2001 Census indicate a changing pattern in the labour force, particularly in terms of education levels and skills. As seen in Figure 2.4, it appears that a large portion of those people that migrated to the City is already skilled and is in possession of a matric certificate or higher qualification. The pressures on the City due to the high levels of unemployment nationally are enormous. The national unemployment rate is 42%. Figure 2.5 shows that the City's current unemployment rate is about 33% and has remained consistently high. However, the City's relatively lower unemployment rate, coupled with potential job opportunities, continues to attract unemployed migrants - placing further pressure on the rate of unemployment in Johannesburg" (p.29)

"Service delivery. Despite the City's huge efforts to deliver services, the rate of people migrating to the City is outpacing the provision of housing and household basic services. This is illustrated by the continuous increase in the number of families living in shacks and the increase in the number of households using candles for lighting. Also, the proportion of households with access to basic services, compared to the total number of households, appears to be decreasing. For example, although over 200 000 additional families received electricity between 1996 and 2001, the percentage of households with electricity has decreased from 86% to 79%" (p.36)

"CONCLUSION. Johannesburg is undoubtedly South Africa's largest and most prosperous City, endowed with world-class infrastructure and relatively high levels of human capital. However, continuing urbanisation and in-migration, poverty, high levels of unemployment and access to basic services confront the City. This Integrated Development Plan (IDP) seeks to reinforce the City's strengths and address its challenges" (p.37)

City of Johannesburg

Ch.5: Sectoral Strategies

Water Services Plan: "Challenges. The challenge is to determine a strategy to meet the exceedingly high short-term growth in water demand resulting from the high population growth rates. This high population growth rate is possibly due to in-migration from other areas, including foreign countries, and is a further indication of a higher than expected economic growth rate. Previous estimates of population growth rates were around 1,8% per annum, but the last census data reflects an annual growth rate of 4,4%" (p.69)

Housing: "Poverty, urbanisation and population growth. The rate of urbanization, natural population growth and poverty must be factored in the determination of statistical population growth and future projections. Johannesburg is showing rapid growth of in-migration trends and patterns with a present 97% urbanisation growth rate in comparison to other cities. These characteristics are a potential threat to the newly formulated City's development frameworks, visions as well as limited resources to implement change" (p.72)

"Conversion of single sex hostels. The central premise of the programme is to convert single sex hostels into a mixed form of accommodation. Primarily and characteristically, the City intends to get rid of the historical single sex hostels, which typify symbols of migratory labour and apartheid. Upgrading programmes are in the pipeline in Madala and Nobuhle hostels in Alexandra. Other hostels that are undergoing a facelift are the Van Beek, Meadowlands, Diepkloof and Helen Joseph" (p.75)

Ch.7: City Plans

Office of the City Manager: "CONTEXT. The Vision of the Office of the City Manager is to "To provide oversight, integration and delivery of strategic priorities to advance the world-class African City. Johannesburg is the largest metropolitan area in South Africa. It is home to 3,225,810 people in 1,006,903 households. The city generates 16% of South Africa's wealth and is recognised as South Africa's premier business location. This has contributed to migration patterns that have resulted in increases in the population of the city and consequent increases in demands for service. The vision of building an African World Class City has also meant that the city is focused on promoting social and economic development. Within this context, the effective management of the city is thus of critical importance" (p.183)

City Parks: "Increasing demographic mobility and the demand for housing currently undermines the sustainability of future conservation areas. New infrastructure supply and business developments which supports urban growth further threatens existing limited conservation areas. These trends contributed extensively to significant reductions in plant and animal species restricted to such conservation areas" (p.214)

Metrobus: Metrobus is a company providing a bus public transport service to the community of Johannesburg.
"CHALLENGES. There are key challenges that Metrobus faces, some of which were briefly mentioned above. These are very specific macro environmental challenges recognised by the company and are listed below: Demographics: Impact on HIV/AIDS on population growth; Migration of people from other areas to the inner city and surrounding areas" (p.267)

City of Johannesburg

Ch.10: Performance Management System

"The Human Development Agenda (HDA) has been initiated to create a policy framework through which the City can begin to tackle issues regarding poverty and quality of life, in a substantive way. It is envisaged that when completed, the agenda will consider how best to assist and empower specific vulnerable groups in the City - including women, children, youth and migrants" (p.317)

Overview:
"South African cities are faced with particular challenges linked to the legacy of apartheid, delayed urbanisation and political transformation" (p18)

"Latest census figures suggest that the process of urbanisation is escalating and this has been demonstrated most vividly by the 20% increase in the Gauteng population" (p19)

"The growth of cities was historically truncated by mechanisms to inhibit black urbanisation and whilst this process ultimately collapsed under the weight of urbanisation pressure, cities were slow to respond to the new challenge" (p19)

"**Addressing the condition of the north defining the developmental approach.** The dualistic tension in Tshwane between North and South is one of the developmental characteristics of the city and thus virtually defines itself as a priority strategic issue. Greater Pretoria has for decades been critiqued for its inability to incorporate the dense peri-urban dormitory settlements on its border (a consequence of past influx control policies) some of which were located within the former Bophuthatswana Bantustan. The municipal demarcation has created the institutional basis for addressing the effects of past urban policies. It is therefore also to be expected that addressing the condition of the North to be a priority political challenge and legitimate electoral expectation." (p38)

"The key developmental challenge is therefore to address the needs of the North by:
· avoiding unsustainable provision of municipal services;
· providing services households can afford by moderating the levels of services;
· concentrating on investing in communal facilities and infrastructure;
· encouraging visible public investment that generates efficiencies through concentrating developments within emerging urban nodes;
· refining tariff and property tax structures that allows optimum distribution of resources;
· bias productive investment to increase access to opportunity, mobility and job creation in SMME and labour intensive enterprises; and
· implementing efficiencies to manage the total cost of municipal services" (p39)

City of Johannesburg

Ch.2 Status Quo Analysis

"The major causes of structural unemployment (see Table 11) are embedded in historical and present political, institutional, socio-economic and economic conditions. It must be understood that structural unemployment is a long-term phenomenon caused by many factors….Furthermore, the job market, education and training initiatives and labour mobility were influenced by biased apartheid policies. Over decades the changes in the South African production structure (e.g. declining primary sector contributions to employment and the GDP) also exacerbated the unemployment situation" (p.60)

Major challenges & threats:

"**Poor Regional Mobility**: The "CTMM-area" lacks an efficient regional based mobility routing system. The eastern areas of CTMM are reasonably well serviced by road systems (N1, R28 and R21); however, these serve less than half the population. In the west, where more than 50% of the population and the majority of the poor live, there are no major routes. Whatever systems there are, are often incomplete" (p62)

"**The Brain Drain**: One of the problems created by globalization has been the increased mobility of skills. Although it has not been adequately quantified, empirical evidence indicates that there has been a significant brain drain, particularly amongst the more highly skilled sectors. The challenge for the LED is to facilitate the development of a skills training process with a dynamic supportive mentoring programme which is implemented across all sectors of its operation." (p.63)

Spatial analysis:

"The spatial consequences of apartheid can be summarised as follows:

o the legacy is one of polarisation between the majority of the city's inhabitants – mainly impoverished black people residing in the remote north-western areas (along the periphery of the previous homelands and almost 50 km from the city centre) - and the relatively affluent, predominantly white population in the south and east, living conveniently close to economic opportunities;

o the problems and needs of people in these peripheral areas are related to poverty, unemployment or low incomes, inaccessibility to jobs, services and amenities, inadequate and insufficient housing and high rates of HIV/AIDS infection;

o the income gap between the poor and the rich is increasing, thus entrenching polarisation;

o the spatial gap is also increasing, as new economic opportunities are developing even further away from the city centre to the south and east around the decentralised nodes;

o the transportation system is not sustainable – it uses close to 30% of national transportation subsidies;

o a huge rural reservoir of people still to be urbanised is living in the apartheid era's "homelands" on Tshwane's periphery." (p65)

"No decentralised nodes developed in the outlying areas to the north. These areas are still dependant on the Inner City for the majority of their needs. The distance and inaccessible location of poor neighbourhoods highlights their dislocation and marginalisation since they have the lowest provision of social facilities, the longest travelling times and the highest population density. These are also the areas that are growing at the fastest rate (population growth). This situation complicates the lives of the majority of residents. In addition, the present situation can only be maintained" (p.66)

Tshwane

"A significant number of people choose to reside in Tshwane (due to its factual and perceived advantages in terms of liveability) and work in Johannesburg (as it offers more economic opportunities). This is also part of a larger international trend towards a more mobile urban community. This has, in part, contributed to the expansion of residential areas in the southern and south-eastern parts of the metropolitan area, to the extent that development is now even spreading beyond Tshwane's borders (and the provincial Development Boundary) into the neighbouring Kungwini municipal area" (p67)

"The proximity to the North-West and Limpopo Provinces results in a constant influx of unskilled and semi-skilled labour from these areas into Tshwane. These people generally tend to settle informally in the northern part of Tshwane which acts as a "transitional zone" for the first wave of urbanisation. The migratory characteristics of the people in these areas influence the type of facilities that should be and are provided and the level of services that should be considered. The management of this area is problematic as it is affected by different sets of legislation and different approaches from the provincial governing bodies. Provincial coordination is necessary to assist the local authority in managing these cross-border areas" (pp.67-8)

Threats and Opportunities related to Tshwane's Environment:

"Population growth and urbanization can lead to greater pressure on environmental resources such as water and open space. Timeous planning is required to provide adequate infrastructure, especially in informal settlements where lack of infrastructure leads to water, soil and air pollution. The current growth rate of informal houses is 18,6%. In view of the fact that 35% of total households within Tshwane are informal, this becomes a significant issue in the promotion of environmental sustainability" (p80)

Ch.6: IDP projects phase

"**Local Government: Municipal Property Rates Bill.** Section 16 of the Bill reads as follows: "Constitutionally impermissible rates (1) In terms of section 229(2)(a) of the Constitution, a municipality may not exercise its power to levy rates on property in a way that would materially and unreasonably prejudice – (a) national economic policies; (b) economic activities across its boundaries; or (c) the national mobility of goods, services, capital or labour" (p.158)

Ch.7:Integrated Plans, Policies and Programmes

"**Disaster Management Plan.** Due to poverty, population growth and rapid urbanization, the vulnerability to disasters has increased. A lack of infrastructure and certain essential services as well as a lack of public awareness, are all factors contributing to disasters. One or more of these factors are present in many communities within Tshwane. Rapid urbanization has already started to exert considerable pressure on Tshwane's infrastructure and there is a large increase in societal conflict, crime and health hazards. The Disaster Management function will ensure that vulnerable communities are identified and multi-sector projects can then be prioritised to address community needs" (p.262)

Tshwane	Ch.9:Assessment of the First Revised IDP **Spatial Development Framework.** "Issue: Present and possible future population movements to, from and within the municipality have been studied and the spatial implications of these for the provision of services and the creation of jobs determined" "Assessment: A detailed analysis of the present and possible future population movements to, from and within the municipality has been done, including its implications on service provision such as water and sanitation, disaster" (p477) Annexure B: IDP Needs Register "ward 418; Need: housing; Community input/wish/request: Proper control of influx of refugees" (p.679) "ward 1234, 1240; need: land invasion & informal settlement management; Community input/wish/request: moving of illegal immigrants to formal housing" (p.783) "ward 2474; need: health & welfare; Community input/wish/request: Homelessness due to HIV/AIDS, and refugees" (p.898)
Ekurhuleni IDP Review (2004)	Section 4: Infrastructure Services 4.1. Municipal Infrastructure "Threats: Uncoordinated influx of people/ population growth" (p.491) SECTION 5 : COMMUNITY SERVICES 5.1. PUBLIC SAFETY "Threats: Illegal immigrants" (p.569) "Threats: Rapid urbanization" (p.569) 5.2. HOUSING "Threat: Growing population/increase in families qualifying for subsidies/uncontrolled settlement formation" (p.623) 5.3. HEALTH AND SOCIAL DEVELOPMENT "Opportunities: Social: Immigration: repatriation of income" "Threat: Rapid urbanization" (p.665)

Cape Town Draft Integrated Development Plan 2004/05 (Mar 2004)

Part C: Our Vision, Goals & Strategies

"The six interrelated strategies are proposed as the starting point for our City development approach:

1. Shifting the development emphasis from the periphery to the urban core.
2. Upgrading existing settlements to places of dignity and opportunity.
3. Building competitive advantage.
4. Facilitating sustainable job creation for all.
5. Building cohesive self-reliant communities.
6. Improving access and mobility" (p16)

"**Strategy 1: Shifting growth to the urban core:** The first strategy is to shift the weight of urban growth from the periphery of the City towards the established urban core through facilitating mixed use, mixed income, high-density development in well-located and accessible areas that are already serviced by current infrastructure. Note that the term "urban core" means all parts of the City with good infrastructure and good access to economic opportunity and amenities, not only the central city around the Cape Town CBD. Housing and service delivery interventions for the poor over the past decade have resulted in large dormitory settlements of low-cost mass housing on the urban periphery, far from opportunity. This has had many benefits but has also had some negative and unintended consequences. These include the lack of employment and recreational opportunities, long travelling times and the reinforcement of the segregation of the City along racial and income lines. This combination of factors tends to trap people in poverty and imposes massive long-term social costs. There is real potential to turn this situation around. Cape Town is unique in having a number of well-located strategic land parcels that are owned by the State, in relatively close proximity to areas of economic activity. These strategically located land parcels offer a number of development opportunities. These include the creation of new suburbs which integrate relatively high density housing in mixed use, mixed income developments. These opportunities can only be unlocked in partnership with other spheres of government, the private sector and local communities. This strategy is necessary to create opportunities for lower income families to live in better-located areas, close to economic activity and social amenities." (pp.18-19)

"**Strategy 6: Improving access and mobility**: This strategy involves improving the access of all citizens to key work and recreational opportunities through integrated transport management, investment in passenger transport and improving Southeast – Northwest linkages in particular. There has been a major underinvestment in transport infrastructure over an extended period and this is a major constraint to making our City more inclusive and more productive or competitive. On average, 66% of the City's population are reliant on public transport to access economic and social opportunities. Most poor residents are almost entirely dependent on public transport. However, public transport is currently in a state of decline, with severe economic and social implications for all of Cape Town's citizens" (p.33)

Annexure 1: Integrating Frameworks

"The City population is growing faster than the national average as people from rural areas, and other, less-successful urban areas, come in search of opportunity and a better life. The City lacks the resource base to provide for the flood of new, largely poor, immigrants – many of whom are unable to find work in our slow economy" (p.44)

Cape Town Draft Integrated Development Plan 2004/05 (Mar 2004)

"**Addressing consequences of the social transition.** More people are moving to the urban areas. Households are shrinking in size and consequently household numbers are increasing. The end of apartheid has led to a new "Great Trek" which ends in the cities. At the same time, the economy is undergoing structural change. There are fewer jobs for less-skilled people, fewer jobs in manufacturing, balanced by some expansion in the tertiary sector – including informal trading. The National Spatial Development Perspective (NSDP), which anticipated much of the social transition, provides a framework for government to focus its efforts on localities that will have the greatest impact in terms of development and poverty alleviation. In these areas, programmes that stimulate economic activity have the most potential to succeed although, given the high numbers of new migrants particularly in urban areas, government will also have to dramatically increase its provision of basic services, skills development and social grants to ease the transition. Further, within these areas, there will also be a need to place greater emphasis on overcoming the spatial disjuncture between home and work by promoting more compact designs that increase residential densities and reduce long-distance commuting. The NSDP will therefore assist government in dealing with the social transition by focusing its activities where it will achieve most impact. In addition to ongoing economic programmes, a massive Public Works Programme is critical. The challenge is to ameliorate the social and other costs of the transition. From a city perspective, the need is to engage National and Provincial Government on these spatial and sectoral issues, which already inform much of Cape Town's strategy for the future" (pp.45-6)

Annexure 3: Financial Framework
"**External factors**: Some of the pertinent external issues affecting the financial viability of the City include:... migration to urban areas" (p.67)

"The growth rate in the City is above the national norm, however, employment opportunities are not being created at the same rate. The growth factors predicted at National Government level will have to be achieved or succeeded in the Western Cape as a whole to provide sufficient opportunities for the economically active population. The City thus takes cognisance of the current migration statistics, employment and poverty levels and general economy to determine the payment threshold that the communities can bear. The limited resources available to the City have to be effectively spread, and value must be added to communities through the efficient application of public funds. Prioritisation is thus given to projects where there is visible usage of public funds to encourage future active participation of the community in Council-organised meetings and increased levels of payment for services" (p.70)

Integrated Development Plan 2005/2006 (2005)

Ch.1: Process Overview.

'Investing in public transport. The City of Cape Town is working with the Provincial Government of the Western Cape on a range of programmes that will significantly improve public transport. Apart from the innovative Bus Rapid Transit System proposed for the Klipfontein Road Corridor, which is expected to unlock mobility in the south-east quadrant of Cape Town, the City is investing in some major transport infrastructure projects' (p.9)

"The 2005/06 IDP has five themes. These are:

- Integrated human settlement, which incorporates two of themes in the 2004/05 IDP, namely 'shifting growth to the urban core' and 'improving existing settlements'. These themes are more logically grouped as one which looks at strategies for tackling Cape Town's housing and settlement challenges
- Similarly, the themes 'sustainable job creation' and 'building competitive advantage' have been grouped together as one theme that tackles a major challenge, that of growing the economy and sharing its fruits.
- The 'strong communities' theme focuses on improving community cohesion and self-reliance through creating a supportive environment.
- The access and mobility theme focuses on improving the management and operations of transport in the city.
- 'Equitable and effective service delivery' constitutes the fifth theme, in recognition of the need for ongoing investment in basic municipal services and infrastructure, and their extension to all parts of the city' (p.10)

Ch. 2: Situational Analysis and Development Challenges

Population Growth and Migration: 'The ongoing growth in the number of households in Cape Town mean that backlogs in housing and service delivery remain high despite a significant increase in the delivery of houses and basic services. While there have been significant increases in the number of households having access to services, there have been no or only slight increases in the percentage of households having access to these services. In other words, despite the significant investment in basic services and the real improvement in quality of life this has delivered for many Capetonians, the efforts have only just kept pace with household growth. The growth in the number of households is partly attributable to the movement of significant numbers of people into the city. It is estimated that 48,000 poor people move into Cape Town each year, implying that an additional 14,000 households need housing and services. While the growth in population adds to the backlog in services, it is an inevitable result of urbanisation and economic development. The priority for city management is thus that improved management of growth in order to integrate new migrants into the city as quickly as possible in terms of accessing services, housing and economic opportunities. Managing urban growth also implies working with other municipalities, particularly district municipalities, in order to better understand and manage the challenge of migration' (pp.11-12)

Key Development Challenges

'While there have been significant investments and successes in the past decade, these have not succeeded in fundamentally shifting Cape Town's development path. More rapid progress in improving Cape Town's development indicators have been constrained by population growth...' (p.14)

Ch.7: Access and Mobility

'To improve access and mobility in Cape Town, there is a need to transform and restructure the current private car, commuter oriented transport system and implement a new model that focuses on the contribution of different modes of transport to the development of the city. Currently, the city is grappling with the pressure of growing demand for access and mobility due to a growing population and increasing tourism. The increase in demand is not being met by the current investment in transport, especially in public transport. This has resulted in worsening traffic, congestion and the deterioration of the public transport service. Inadequate infrastructure, low capacity and poor traffic control and enforcement are contributing to the growth in traffic congestion with high costs in terms of hours lost in traffic and long commuting times. Increasing travel times also means increasing energy consumption which aggravates pollution. Under-investment in new transport infrastructure in both public transport and roads is compounded by inadequate maintenance and degradation of existing assets, resulting in a decrease in the level of service and poor safety standards. Poor access and mobility has serious impact on the city's economy, with areas of job opportunities, economic development and housing developments located outside the established radial transport corridors (both rail and road based corridors). An integrated transport network is required to link activities and people. The current public transport system and service is unreliable and infrequent with tidal morning and evening peaks, yet over 60% of commuters depend on the rail, bus and taxi service. A large number of of the urban poor who live on the outskirts of the city have limited access and choice with regard to the mode of transport most suited to their access and mobility needs" (p.)

The key strategies for improving access and mobility are:

Programme 1: Governance and institutional arrangements (establish Transport Authority)

Programme 2: Improved public transport (establish Public Transport Management Structure)

Programme 3: Integrated transport corridors (Klipfontein Rapid Bus Transit Corridor, N2 Gateway Project)

Programme 4: Improved transport network and infrastructure (Public Transport Strategy, CCTV & Surveillance Strategy, implantation of a dedicated Public Transport Law Enforcement unit, upgrading public transport facilities and infrastructure)

Programme 5: Promote non-motorised transport (City-wide strategy, review Dial-a-Ride Transport Service)

Integrated Development Plan 2005/2006 (2005)

Integrated Development Plan 2005/2006 (2005)	**Ch.9: Spatial Framework** 'Challenges. Spatially, Cape Town faces serious problems on many fronts. The structure and form of the city generates enormous amounts of movement, at great cost to the public purse in infrastructure, energy consumed and pollution generated. Traffic congestion is increasing and for those who cannot afford a car, life is inconvenient and expensive. Public transport is inefficient and it is difficult to switch from one mode of transport to another, and some parts of the city are not accessible. Poverty and inequality are made worse by this since it is the poor who are the most affected...Inadequate shelter and homelessness are growing problems and the city's magnificent natural environment is constantly under threat of indiscriminate development' (p.34) **Ch.10: Financial Plan** *'Financial factors affecting the City's financial planning.* Apart from international factors some of the key driver and challenges that will impact on City resources include:....in-migration from rural areas' (p.40) **Appendix 2: Sector Plans – HIV, AIDS and TB** "Factors fuelling HIV/AIDS in Cape Town:...migrant labour" (p.75) "Factors fuelling TB in Cape Town:...urbanisation with resultant overcrowding" (p.75)
eThekwini IDP 2003-2007 (June 2003)	No mention of migration issues

Reviewed IDP 2003-07: Review period 2004-2005 (June 2004):	**Ch.6: Health and Empowered Citizens** **"6.2.1.4 Vulnerable groups.** The municipality comprises diverse communities with diverse needs. Certain groups of people have greater risks of exposure to vulnerability. For social and biological reasons, women are more vulnerable than men. Poor people are more vulnerable than the better off; adolescents are more vulnerable than adults; and young girls are more vulnerable than young boys. Special risk groups include migrants and refugees, especially those uprooted by conflict or natural disaster; street children; girls and women who are sexual exploited and trafficked; and intravenous drug users. Responding to the interests and specific needs of these groups requires a coordinated and integrated approach from all key roleplayers within the Municipality" (p37)
Nelson Mandela IDP 2002-2005 (2ⁿᵈ Ed)(2003)	**Foreword by the Executive Mayor:** "The Metro currently provides various curative and preventative health services through 41 fixed and 15 mobile clinics. In order to provide an adequate service the Metro needs to build 4 new clinics per annum, redistribute mobile clinics to better serve remote areas and employ an additional 93 nurses. Increasing the health of the citizens has a direct impact on the productivity of the labour force, but also makes the city more attractive for inward migration from less served areas" (p.i) **Housing & Land Portfolio: Implementation Framework** "5 Year Developmental Priority Strategies:12. Consideration of other special housing programmes pertaining to special groups" "Strategic Priority 2003/04: Investigate programmes to effect the delivery of special projects e.g. Immigrants, street-children H.I.V orphans" (p.54) **Infrastructure, Engineering, Electricity and Energy Portfolio:** "The envisaged economic and tourism development plans of the metro, the increasing population as a result of migration presents a danger to the infrastructure and town planning of the metro. Also the physical expansion of the metro in the periphery of its boundaries creates mobility and transportation obstacles to the affected residents. These obstacles could in the long term stifle the economic growth that is intended for the area. The need for improved long-term development of public transport and road infrastructure systems has become urgent. The portfolio must investigate and develop a costed proposal in that regard" (p.61) **Budget and Treasury Portfolio:** "Because of limited financial resources faced by our municipality and ongoing urbanization challenges that continue to put strain on infrastructural, service delivery and developmental projects, it is imperative that the Budget and Treasury Portfolio identifies revenue and resources beyond our traditional funding streams. In-house capacity must be established to identify a variety of sources of funding catering for a wide range of developmental projects, and not just restricted to infrastructure and service delivery requirements" (p.150)

Appendix 3: The Coverage of Migration in Namibia's Poverty Reduction Strategy (1998), National Poverty Reduction Action Programme (NPRAP, 2001) and Second National Development Plan (NDP2, 2002)

Country	Priority Public Actions
Namibia *Poverty Reduction Strategy for Namibia (1998)*	**Foreword** 'Poverty is concentrated among groups, which historically have been disadvantaged. Consequently, as the 1993/94 Namibia Household Income and Expenditure Survey suggests, poverty is disproportionately to be found among rural people, especially those in remote locations and other areas which were subject to systematic underinvestment; female-headed households; youth; elderly and disabled; and recent migrants into marginalized urban areas' (p.1) **1. Background and Goals** No mention of migration issues. **2. Namibia's Daunting Challenge** 'Namibia's 1993/4 Household income and expenditure survey found that cash wages (from formal and informal employment) were the main source for 44 percent of households, and subsistence farming for 35 percent. Pensions and remittances provide important supplements.' (p.6) 'Third, population is growing at a very rapid rate. Between 1970 and 1997, population has grown from 700,000 to 1.7 million. If population continues to grow at the current rate, the number of Namibians will exceed 3 million by the year 2020. Without a coherent and practical strategy for poverty reduction, the result of rapid population growth could be a rise in both rural distress and urban dysfunction. Windhoek's population, for example, has risen from 61,000 in 1970, to over 180,000 in 1995. Somewhat over two-thirds of this increase has come from migration, with over half of the migrants coming from the four regions in the North-Central. By 2020 Windhoek's population is estimated to be well in excess of 600,000 people. Yet already in 1996 - even with the world's most stringent system of urban water management, re-use and scarcity pricing - Windhoek appeared to be in imminent danger of running out of water' (p.6) **3. A prosperous Namibia: Realizing the Longrun Vision** 'In the long-run, a prosperous Namibia will have a very different economy than it does today. The agricultural base is too weak to offer a sustainable basis for prosperity. So a quarter century from now, the large majority of the country's inhabitants (by then more than 3 million) are likely to have moved into urban centres: Windhoek; Walvis Bay/Swakopmund; Ondangwa/Oshakati; Rundu; Katima Mulilo; and perhaps others. The challenge for an integrated strategy of poverty reduction is to ensure that by that time, the country's urban centers are capable of providing good jobs at good wages. Achieving this calls for immediate sustained efforts on two fronts - laying the foundations for transforming Namibia into an industrial society, and investing in people's education and health' (p.7)

Country	Priority Public Actions
Namibia *Poverty Reduction Strategy for Namibia (1998)*	**3.1 A transport and manufacturing hub** No explicit mention of migration issues. **3.2 Investing in people** No explicit mention of migration issues. **3.2.1 Education** No explicit mention of migration issues. **3.2.2 Health** No explicit mention of migration issues. **4. Meeting the Challenge of the Present** **4.1 Some Near-term Opportunities for Poverty-reducing Income Generation** **4.1.1 Agriculture** No explicit mention of migration issues. **4.1.2 Tourism** No explicit mention of migration issues. **4.1.3 Small and medium enterprises** No explicit mention of migration issues. **4.2 Strengthening Namibia's safety net** **4.2.1 Labour-intensive public works** No explicit mention of migration issues. **4.2.2 Strengthening grant-based transfer programs** No explicit mention of migration issues. **5. Making the Most of Public Resources** No explicit mention of migration issues. **6. Institutional Framework for Strategy Implementation** No explicit mention of migration issues.

Country	Priority Public Actions
National Poverty Reduction Action Programme 2001-2005 (NPRAP, Oct 2001)	**Chapter 1: Introduction** 'The gap in average rural and urban income and living standard gives a strong incentive for rural-urban migration as evidenced by the growth of informal settlements in peri-urban areas of almost all urban centres in the country.' (p.19) 'Along with subsistence farmers, poverty can be found amongst farm and domestic workers. Furthermore, elderly and people with disabilities, young women and men, and recent migrants into marginalised urban areas are disproportionately affected by poverty. Finally, many poor households rely on the state pension as an important income source' (p.20) 'Male migration away from many rural areas has increased the number of female-headed households. These households face additional risks and constraints due to their more limited labour supply, fewer wage earners and the difficulty for women to obtain credit and other productive resources. Men, on the other hand, must often travel greater distances to find work, must accept lower paying jobs and suffer the loss to self-esteem of not being able to provide for the needs of the family' (p.22) **Chapter 2: A Prosperous Namibia** **2.1. A transport and manufacturing hub** No mention of migration issues. **2.2. Investing in people - Education** 'In the northern Kunene Region, mobile schools were introduced as a pilot programme in 1998 with the support of NAMAS. These mobile schools follow the pastoral nomads. The programme improves accessibility and raises awareness in the communities for the importance of education.' (p.32)

Country	Priority Public Actions
National Poverty Reduction Action Programme 2001-2005 (NPRAP) Oct 2001)	**2.3. Health** 'In 1996, the Government adopted the National Population Policy for Sustainable Human Development. This policy aims to 'contribute to the improvement of the standard of living and quality of life of the people of Namibia—through the harmonisation of the dynamics of Namibia's population (its growth rate, age and sex structure, migration and urbanisation) with the country's resource potential in order to accomplish development objectives' (p.36) 'The National Population Policy for Sustainable Human Development affects all regions and involves a number of central government ministries, regional councils, regional development co-ordinating committees and other stakeholders involved in its implementation. It contributes to the reduction of poverty in Namibia by improving the quality of life of the people through population and development policies and programmes that are designed to alleviate poverty and promote sustainable development. It also focuses on the improvement of health and welfare services by reducing the incidence of morbidity and mortality, particularly infant, child and maternal mortality and ensuring a balanced development of rural and urban areas in order to prevent excessive urbanisation' (p.37) **Chapter 3: Income Generation** **3.1. Agriculture** No mention of migration issues. **3.2. Tourism** No mention of migration issues. **3.3. Small and medium enterprise development** No mention of migration issues. **Chapter 4: Strengthening Namibia's safety net** **4.1. Labour intensive public works** No mention of migration issues. **4.2. Strengthening grant-based transfer programmes** No mention of migration issues. **Chapter 5: Making the most of public resources** No mention of migration issues. **Chapter 6: Implementation, Monitoring and Review** No mention of migration issues.

Country	Priority Public Actions
National Development Plan (NDP2, 2002) – Chapter 33: Poverty Reduction	**Section 1: Description of the sector** 'The gap in average rural and urban income and living standards gives a strong incentive for rural-urban migration. The result is that informal settlements in the peri-urban areas are on the rise. This is happening in almost every urban centre in the country.' (p.559) 'Furthermore, the elderly and people with disabilities, the youth and recent migrants into marginalised urban areas are disproportionately affected by poverty (p.559) **Section 2: Review of the sector performance during NDP1** No mention of migration issues. **Section 3: Sector mission statement, major sector objectives, targets and performance indicators** No mention of migration issues. **Section 4: Sector strategies** No mention of migration issues. **Section 5: Sector programmes** No mention of migration issues.

Appendix 4: The Coverage of Migration in Swaziland's Poverty Reduction Strategy Action Plan (PRSAP, 2005)

Country	Priority Public Actions
Swaziland *Draft Poverty Reduction Strategy and Action Plan (PRSAP, Mar 2005)*	**Chapter 1: Introduction** No mention of migration issues. **Chapter 2: Status of Poverty in Swaziland** • 2.3. *Sources of Income for the Poor:* 'According to SHIES of 1995, the rural poor generate 75% of their income from wages and self-employment in business compared to farm income, which generates 12%. Other sources of income were remittances (2%) and other income (9%). These findings show that the labour market has been the main source of income for the poor and that they need the right skills to find the jobs. Prospects for employment in the country and in neighbouring countries, especially South Africa are, however, dwindling. In 1990, there were 16,500 Swazi migrant workers employed in the South African mines compared to about 13,000 in 1997' (p.20) **Chapter 3: Policy Framework for Poverty Reduction** **3.3 National Policy Priorities** **3.3.6 Investment in rural infrastructure to increase rural productivity** 'This will not only boost the creation of employment opportunities but will reduce the rate of rural-urban migration by increasing opportunities of investment in the rural sector. The government will therefore continue to invest in rural roads and bridges, power supply, rural water supply, rural electrification, industrial parks and telecommunication' (p.35)

Country	Priority Public Actions
Swaziland *Draft Poverty Reduction Strategy and Action Plan* (PRSAP, Mar 2005)	**Chapter 4: Macro-economic Environment** **4.2. Macro-economic Policy Environment** **4.2.9. Strategies for 'Poverty-Conscious' Trade Reforms** following strategies will be adopted in order to facilitate trade reform: • Facilitate the mobility of labour between and within regions and the neighbouring countries; (p.49) **Chapter 5: Empowering the Poor to Generate Income** **5.2. Agriculture** **5.2.1. Increasing Income from Agricultural Production** 'It is therefore clear that to earn income from agriculture, productivity of SNL must considerably be raised beyond household consumption so as to produce surplus for sale. Only 12% of income is generated from farming indicating the non-viability of farming as an income generating activity. Most households rely on remittances to meeting their needs' (p.56) **5.3. Creating Employment Opportunities** 'The drastic and fast increase in unemployment is the major reason for the impoverishment and deepening inequalities among the Swazi population. The poor are more vulnerable to redundancies and job losses as they hold low paying, low skill and seasonal jobs. They are also very dependent on employment income and remittances' (p.61) **5.3.1. Current employment environment** 'Although Swaziland has grown in the past, this growth has not translated into the creation of quality jobs. The national unemployment rate is very high, calculated at 29% (SHIES 2001) with the youth at more than 40%. This development is in direct relationship with the decline in economic growth driven by the poor performance of the agricultural sector; low levels of foreign direct investment; lack of skilled man-power; loss of skilled personnel who leave the country in search for greener pastures; poor infrastructure in rural areas compared to urban infrastructure; closure and the restructuring of major export-oriented companies. Furthermore, the structure and size of industries which have become more capital intensive has not provided solutions to the unemployment problem. Unfortunately, these developments have coincided with a decline in migrant labour opportunities in the South African mines' (p.62)

Country	Priority Public Actions
Swaziland *Draft Poverty Reduction Strategy and Action Plan* (PRSAP, Mar 2005)	**5.3.6. Promoting Tourism** 'In order to create more employment opportunities, there will be a fervent drive to promote community tourism and thus reduce the need to migrate to the cities' (p.66) **5.3.12. Support to the Informal Sector** 'The informal sector has continued to be the primary source of livelihood for the unemployed and poor, especially women. It has become the only solace for most people, especially women, school leavers, returnees from migrant employment, redundant, unskilled and disadvantaged members of society' (p.68) **5.6. Strategies for Supporting the Informal Sector** 'Providing training and inspections on health and quality requirements. This will also involve the regulation (or possible elimination) of sub-standard goods from foreign countries, through cross-border illegal movements or other unscrupulous means' (p.71) **Chapter 6: Human Capital Development** **6.2. Basic Health** **6.2.8. Provide Effective Basic Health Services** Strategies for preventive health care to be followed will be: v. Remove the urban bias in the provision of health services. 70% of the population live in rural areas and that is where the majority of the poor reside. (p.96)

Country	Priority Public Actions
Swaziland *Draft Poverty Reduction Strategy and Action Plan (PRSAP, Mar 2005)*	**6.3. HIV/AIDS** **6.3.1. The Spread of HIV/AIDS** 'There is only a marginal difference in the prevalence of the pandemic in rural areas (35.9%) and urban areas (40.6%). This could be due to the easy access and high population mobility between regions, across the country and the close interlinkages between rural and urban areas. It could also be due to social and cultural factors that contribute to the spread making the population vulnerable to infection especially women and girls. The prevalence rates for the four regions of Swaziland show no significant differences, although Shiselweni recorded the highest escalation and is also the poorest region with the highest level of absentee heads that work outside the country. Manzini has the highest level of infection at 41.2% and is the richest and most urbanised region in the country' (p.100) **6.3.2. Socio-Economic Impact [of HIV/AIDS]** The migration of family breadwinners in search for income to sustain their households results in the breakdown of family relations, increasing the likelihood of multiple sexual partners and casual partners consequently increasing the risk of HIV infection. In Swaziland, men leave homes in search of employment opportunities, moving to towns and out of the borders to RSA leaving behind their partners. However, according to the 1997 census, women have emerged as migrants as they are predominantly involved in the hawking business (p.102) **6.3.3. HIV/AIDS and Poverty** 'The task of managing the pandemic is a difficult one. There is lack of development of appropriate health promotion centres, home-based programmes and hospices within affected communities. Service related programmes are concentrated in urban communities and donor assistance in this area is limited. A common but diminishing practice in AIDS-affected households is to send some of the orphaned and very young children to extended family members to be cared for. This may be an attribute of the high dependency ratio among the poor whose families are inherently dominated by children and the elderly. The ability of extended families to absorb such stress has been reduced by urbanisation and labour migration. As the number of orphans increases, the traditional coping mechanisms are weakened. Orphan headed families are becoming prevalent in Swaziland, particularly among poor families' (p.103)

Country	Priority Public Actions
Swaziland *Draft Poverty Reduction Strategy and Action Plan* *(PRSAP, Mar 2005)*	**Chapter 7: Improving the Quality of Life** **7.2. Improving Housing** **7.2.1. Causes of Poor Housing** 'The rapid rate of urban migration in search of employment has led to the mushrooming of sub-standard houses on SNL [Swazi Nation Land] in a very haphazard and unplanned manner. The mushrooming of shabby structures on the outskirts of the country's major towns has skipped the control of local authorities and no one seems to have control or authority over the development of these areas. Moreover, due to the financial gains now attached to land in the outskirts of urban areas, farmland is being sold for the construction of houses and the remaining hectarage, if any, cannot be used for any meaningful and gainful farming activity. This situation has led to increased congestion, poor sanitation and a lot of hunger and malnutrition due to limited potential for income generation on the remaining portions of land' (p.128) **7.2.3. Strategies for Improving Housing Conditions** To enable households to construct and maintain the desired housing units, government shall: • Regulate and formulate laws that control the growth of sub-standard houses and unplanned human settlements in peri-urban areas; • Improve rural conditions to reverse the rapid rate of migration and congestion in the cities; (p.129)

Country	Priority Public Actions
Swaziland *Draft Poverty Reduction Strategy and Action Plan* (PRSAP Mar 2005)	**Chapter 8: Good governance** No mention of migration issues. **Chapter 9: Cross-cutting issues** **9.1. Population Issues** **9.1.2. Population Structure and Characteristics** The distribution of the rural population among the four regions of the country is uneven, with Manzini accounting for the highest %age (31%) and Lubombo the least (19%). Hhohho and Shiselweni each account for 25% of the rural Swazi population. The migration of people between regions is relatively low; however it is very high between rural and urban areas as people search for job opportunities and a means of earning a living. There has been a considerable increase in the rate of urbanisation in the last thirty years, from 14.2% to 23%. More than half of the urban population is concentrated in the two cities of Mbabane and Manzini leading particularly to urban unemployment, emergence of unplanned for human settlements which have no provision for public infrastructure and services, are infested with crime and street children (pp.151-2). The strategic objective of the Poverty Reduction Strategy and Action Plan is therefore to match population growth with factors that determine socially acceptable standards of the quality of life of the population. The underlying principle is that economic development and other related factors should influence the quality of life and provide equitable access to services and resultantly all citizens should have an improved life. Inevitably, population growth will slow down and stabilize at the level commensurate with sustainable development. On its part, the government shall pursue the following mutually supportive strategic objectives with a sharp focus on the poor segments of the Swazi population: • To curb illegal immigration (p.153). **9.1.7. Strategies for Population Right-Sizing** Under the PRSAP the government will continue existing strategies and initiate new ones focused on the poor in the following broad areas: • Strengthen border immigration controls. Improve access to natural resources particularly land; (p.154).

Country	Priority Public Actions
Swaziland *Draft Poverty Reduction Strategy and Action Plan (PRSAP, Mar 2005)*	**9.1.5. Strategic Objective** **9.2. Environment** **9.2.1. Environment and Poverty** 'Three of the most critical environmental problems in Swaziland are soil erosion, deforestation and forest degradation (including both actual loss of trees and the changing composition and structure); and water and air pollution. One of the major causes of these problems is the lack of enforcement of environmental laws, the increasing resident population, which has been accompanied by the unsustainable exploitation of natural resources, overgrazing on communal lands, increasing urbanisation and diminishing farm size. In turn, this has mounted pressure on Swaziland's natural resources' (p.156) **9.2.2.1. Environmental Health** 'The use of shallow pit latrines, buckets and the bush as toilet facilities is therefore a big health hazard that must be addressed with urgency. Another critical problem that has emerged due to the overcrowded human settlements in the outskirts of urban areas is that of poor sanitation, unplanned housing and infrastructure, and no farmland for the people who live in these areas. This exacerbates the poverty problem and contributes to the problems of disease and malnutrition' (p.158) **9.3. Gender Equality** **9.3.5. Gender and Land/Property** 'Land is the main resource for growing food, but evidence shows between that about 40% of households never produce enough in any year. Recent assessments indicate that maize production went down by 40% between 1990 and 2000 further worsening the food situation of poor families. They depend on remittances to buy food packages. FHH are the most affected because they have no head to earn to supplement their food requirements' (p.169) **Chapter 10: Implementation, Monitoring and Evaluation** No mention of migration issues.

Country	Priority Public Actions
Swaziland *Draft Poverty Reduction Strategy and Action Plan* (PRSAP, Mar 2005)	**ACTION PROGRAMME FOR THE REDUCTION OF POVERTY (PRSAP Vol. II)** **Chapter 1: Introduction** **Implementation** 'Government's major role in the PRSAP is that of a facilitator – providing policy environment and basic infrastructure to act as a stimulus for the market economy and expanding opportunities for the poor. Infrastructural improvements include the road network, Information Communications Technology (ICT) and markets which will improve access, facilitate communication and mobility for both urban, rural and commercial institutions and the people. The PRSAP will give priority to the rehabilitation and construction of basic infrastructure to those areas of the country with the largest populations and highest levels of poverty.' (p.16) **Chapter 2: Policy Framework for Poverty Reduction** **2.3. National Policy Priority** **2.3.5. Investment in rural infrastructure to increase rural productivity** 'Rural infrastructure will not only boost the creation of employment opportunities but will reduce the rate of rural-urban migration by increasing opportunities of investment in the rural sector. The government will therefore continue to invest in rural roads and bridges, power supply, rural water supply, rural electrification, industrial parks and telecommunication. Notwithstanding government obligations, investment in infrastructure and telecommunication are not areas of exclusive mandate to the public sector. The private sector will therefore be encouraged to participate wherever feasible in infrastructural investment and private-public partnerships will be greatly encouraged' (p.30). **Chapter 3: Macroeconomic Environment** No mention of migration issues.

Country	Priority Public Actions
Swaziland *Draft Poverty Reduction Strategy and Action Plan (PRSAP, Mar 2005)*	**Chapter 4: Empowering the Poor to Generate Income** **4.4 SME and Microenterprise Development** **Action 42. Provide Investment Incentives in Rural Areas and Promote the Development of SMEs** Poverty can be reduced if investment takes place in rural as well as in urban areas. The Ministry of Enterprises and Employment shall strategically establish additional factory shells in rural areas covering all four regions where economies of scale exist so as to promote investment in rural areas. The Ministry will work in collaboration of other agencies to provide infrastructure that is necessary for SMEs to flourish (p.49). **Chapter 5: Human Capital Development** No mention of migration issues. **Chapter 6: Improving the Quality of Life** No mention of migration issues. **Chapter 7: Ensuring Good Governance** No mention of migration issues. **Chapter 8: Cross Cutting Issues** **8.1. Population Issues** **Action 164. Strengthening Immigration Control** 'The number of illegal immigrants has increased to very concerning levels in Swaziland, thus adding a lot of pressure on the country's social services, natural resources and the economy as a whole. The Department of Immigration shall strengthen their efforts to curb the influx of illegal immigrants. More controls and laws that will ensure the removal and barring of these immigrants will be put in place and enforced' (p.94). **Chapter 9: National Planning and Budget Framework** No mention of migration issues. **Chapter 10: Ongoing Pro-Poor Projects in the Budget** No mention of migration issues. **Chapter 11: Poverty Projects in the Prioritised Action Programme on Poverty Reduction** No mention of migration issues.

www.ingramcontent.com/pod-product-compliance
Lightning Source LLC
Chambersburg PA
CBHW081436270326
41932CB00019B/3223